MW01153957

the right track

the right track

Arena exercises for riders and instructors

•

Sarah Venamore

Trafalgar Square Books

North Pomfret, Vermont

First published in the United States of America in 2007 by
Trafalgar Square Books, North Pomfret, Vermont 05053

Printed by Midas Printing International Limited, China

© Sarah Venamore 2003, 2007
First published in Australia in 2003 by Excalibur Press
First published in Great Britain 2007

ISBN 978-1-57076-369-4

Library of Congress Control Number: 2006911242

The right of Sarah Venamore to be identified as author of this work has been asserted by
her in accordance with the Copyright, Designs and Patents Act 1988

Disclaimer of Liability
The author and publisher shall have neither liability nor responsibility to any person or enti-
ty with respect to any loss or damage caused or alleged to be caused directly or indirectly
by the information contained in this book. While the book is as accurate as the author can
make it, there may be errors, omissions, and inaccuracies.

10 9 8 7 6 5 4 3 2 1

Author's acknowledgements

This collection of exercises is dedicated to the Pony Club parents who regularly give up their Sundays to inspire and train our riders. Your encouragement led me to compile this book.

Thank you also to our fabulous pony club horses who were happy to try these exercises and prove they are possible.

I would also like to thank the following:

I'd like to thank Lyn Cunnew and Kate Prestney for their typesetting and drawings in the first Australian print.

Thank you to the Equestrian Federation of Australia and the Pony Club Association who have added this book to their recommended reading list for instructors.

Thanks to my parents who, with no knowledge of horses, trusted my instincts to work in the horse industry enough to put me through university and send me overseas to get the best education possible.

Finally, to the instructors who have taught me over the last twenty years. Their ideas helped me with my riding and now I am able to pass them on to others in this book.

Foreword

From fun, to dreams, to being a legend, the equestrian of today and tomorrow just *has* to follow a systematic and safe path.

Always as a rider, as an instructor, as a pony club parent, the question is 'where is there an easy to understand systematic approach which embraces fun and dreams at the beginning end of the scale and yet dovetails perfectly into launching ambitions at the top end of the scale?'…

It's my opinion that *The Right Track* written by Sarah Venamore offers exactly that; a pathway that is safe, is fun and leads to dressage skills at the legend end of the scale.

I hope you enjoy this book and I look forward to Olympians of tomorrow talking about their early days and *The Right Track*.

Cheers,

Heath K. Ryan

About the author

Sarah Venamore is an internationally experienced horse-woman. She is renowned amongst her students for the clarity of her teaching, and this book encapsulates the essence of her style.

Sarah's riding career began when she was 16 at a trail riding school owned by John and Janet Anderson in Toowoomba, Queensland, Australia. Following a Diploma in Horse Husbandry from the University of Queensland, Sarah travelled to the United Kingdom to take up a position at the Talland School of Equitation in Cirencester. At Talland, Sarah worked for and studied under Mrs Molly Sivewright and gained her British Horse Society Assistant Instructor Certificate.

After returning home, Sarah took up a position at the Dalson Park Equestrian Centre in Brisbane, Queensland, on advice from equestrienne Sandra Pearson-Adams. Sarah managed and instructed group lessons at the Centre. While in Queensland Sarah also obtained the National Coaching Accreditation Scheme, Equestrian Federation of Australia (EFA), Level 1 General examination.

A move south to the Highlands Equestrian Centre on the Southern Highlands of New South Wales followed, and it was here that Sarah became involved in teaching groups of riders as she trained EFA Level 1 candidates.

After two years Sarah left the Highlands Equestrian Centre to begin her own equestrian coaching business. At the outset she taught privately, until the New South Wales Pony Club Association invited her to undertake the role of State Dressage Coach.

Sarah soon noticed the flagging interest of riders in group lessons facing yet another hour of flat work. It was this experience which led her to create unusual and challenging exercises which would spark interest in riders. She developed these exercises over a long period, and they have proven very effective to improve skill levels while keeping riders engaged. Even the five-year-old students will ask to ride 'The Snowman' or 'Monkey Ears' again.

While some of the exercises in this book have been taught to Sarah during her own training, Sarah has devised the rest herself, refining and improving them. Sarah uses them extensively – and successfully – to hold the interest of young riders as they train at her riding camps. They are presented in an easily usable fashion in this book for all riders and trainers to benefit.

Contents

Note to riders   10
The arena   11
How to use this book   12
Teaching directives   13
Lesson plan for the new instructor   14–17
Glossary of terms   18–1

Warm-up Exercises   21–37
Snowmen   39–49
Monkey Ears   51–63
Circle Exercises   65–75
Chopsticks   77
Egg Exercises   79–83
Cogwheel   85
Bug Eyes   87–89
ABC Logo   91–99
Caterpillar   101
Worm Exercise   103
Turns on the Forehand   105–107
Leg Yielding Exercises   109–111
Canter Shorts   113–117
Straight Line Tracks   119–125
Hourglass   127–133
Looples   135–139
Double Arena Exercises   141–149
Abacus   151–153
Bubble Exercises   155–165
Bubble Letters   167–171
Safety Pin   173–177
Bowtie Exercises   179–181
Butterfly Exercises   183–185
Dominoes   187–189

Index   191

Note to riders

The exercises have been designed for a 20 x 60 metre dressage arena.

The exercises found in the book are designed for quiet horses with some education and the ability to work in company with other horses.

The exercises can be used by individual riders or as a coaching tool (see page 13) and to teach riders to be aware of riding in company with others

The author recommends riding two or three exercises in a one-hour session. The rider should choose a 'warm-up' exercise involving halt or walk (allowing at least ten minutes), then progress to a trotting exercise and, depending on capability, add canter to the 'trot' exercise or find a suitable canter exercise.

It is important to be aware of horse and rider fitness levels to ensure plenty of rest, breaks between exercises and to cool the horse down before dismounting.

NB: The exercises are generally drawn on one rein only. Riders should ensure that equal time is spent on both reins.

If you are in doubt about the position of letters when setting up the arena, try using this little rhyme to remember their order (anti-clockwise from A):

A

Fat

Partially

Black

Ratty

Mother

Cat

Had

Some

Eleven

Voracious

Kittens

How to use this book

The Right Track is divided into groups of patterns starting with relatively easy exercises and progressing to a greater degree of difficulty as the standard of riding improves.

Each exercise is classified to make it both rider and instructor friendly...

Gait: The suggested gait for the exercise. It may be downgraded (e.g. walk) or upgraded if needed.

Code	Degree of difficulty
∪	Easy – walk, trot, canter
∪∪	Novice – lengthen, shorten, leg yielding
∪∪∪	More advanced – lateral, medium and collected work

No. of riders: The suggested number of riders for the exercise can accommodate.
If the riders are capable, it may be possible to have more riders in a group.

Aims: What the riders are trying to achieve on completion of the exercise.

Instructions: The explanation of the exercise.

Note: Any further important information riders and instructors may need.

Refer to the **Glossary of Terms** for clarification of the terminology used in the exercises.

Teaching directives

When organising a lesson plan the instructor should:

- have information about the group they are about to teach to enable them to choose a suitable lesson plan;
- have an objective for that lesson, e.g. to improve riders' sitting trot;
- be able to demonstrate the exercise they are planning to teach;
- be able to change the plan if the group is more advanced or less advanced than first?thought.

When teaching, be motivational and encouraging, especially in large group lessons, as there can be limited room to move and riders may need help to work in a confined area. On completion of the lesson constructively criticise each horse and rider combination and finish with positive reinforcement.

When teaching, the instructor must stand outside the arena:

- to observe the whole ride from a safety aspect (e.g. distances between each rider are safe, and horse/rider combinations are not likely to be kicked);
- to observe both sides of the riders;
- to assess that the exercise is appropriate for the level of the ride.

The instructor must also take into consideration the direction of wind (behind the instructor so the voice travels further) and position of the sun (so the instructor is not looking directly into the sun and the ride can be clearly seen).

All exercises commence across the centre line at the halt where the instructor explains the lesson plan. The author suggests drawing the diagrams in the sand arena so the riders can see the exercise clearly and comprehend the task required of them. Failing this the instructor can walk (or run!) the exercise on foot to demonstrate.

When instructed, riders proceed straight ahead at the walk to the long side of the large arena track where the exercise commences. The exercise will allow time for the instructor to make corrections to individuals whilst keeping the whole ride working. The instructor should devote equal time to each rider, working on the horse and rider partnership as a whole. Combine rider positional corrections with corrections as to how the horse is travelling, to improve the partnership.

Usually the ride is led by the larger moving horses followed by the smaller ones down to pony size. This allows the ponies to 'catch up' by cutting corners. In these exercises, the ride will usually be moving independently around the arena and if riders find themselves catching up too quickly, they will need to practise some shorter steps. Once there is a space, move forward into the original tempo.

One-hour lesson plan
– for the new instructor

If you're new to teaching, you may find the following information very useful.

Following is an example of how to conduct a group riding lesson using two exercises from *The Right Track* within a one-hour session.

Lesson group: 6 students
Choice of exercise: Halts across the Centre Line (page 23)
                     ABC Logo (page 91)

Halts across the Centre Line

Introduction: Introduce yourself to the ride and commence the gear check of each rider whilst asking their names and the history of the horse/rider partnership.

Explanation: Explain to the ride the warm-up exercise. The ride will commence on the large arena track on the left rein and when it is safe to do so, the riders individually turn across the arena and halt as they reach the centre line. Hold the halt for four seconds (unless waiting for a space on the large arena) then ride a straight line to the large arena track and track left.

Demonstration: Whilst explaining the exercise, draw the diagram in the ground so the riders understand the direction and the exercise plan. Explain the necessity of one horse's distance between each rider for safety.

Execution: Nominate a leader (who responds by saying 'I am leading' so that the ride knows who will lead the group to the track). Once all the riders are travelling large in walk, the instructor begins to watch each rider's position and individually corrects them. The priority here is the rider's centre of gravity (keeping the ear, shoulder, hip and heel line).

Draw the diagram in the sand so the riders understand the direction and the exercise plan.

When the rider is straight, check the horse's straightness (spine alignment with the track the rider is travelling).

Keep the ride at walk as part of the warm-up until you are satisfied with rider and horse corrections.

Then the exercise may be commenced at walk or trot depending on the length of warm-up needed and the level of the riders.

Watch a few halt transitions through walk first, to check the basics are correct (i.e. that the horse pushes forward to a straight halt whilst staying on the bit or at least not pulling into the rider's hands).

The rider halts for four seconds and if there is a space on the outside track, pushes forward through walk to trot and upon reaching the large arena, tracks left.

If there is not a space because the rest of the ride is trotting large, the rider may halt as long as is necessary to create a safe space for himself and his horse. The instructor should be checking there is at least one horse's length between each horse/rider.

Once the ride is achieving some good halts command them to stay large and change rein by nominating a new leader and changing rein across the next diagonal line (e.g. from F through X to H). Then work through the same transitions on the right rein.

Aim: Look for smooth transitions into and out of trot, walk and halt with the horse on the bit. If the riders are not yet riding their horses on the bit, make sure they ride the horses straight into the transitions. As the ride warms up, ask for more accurate transitions thus working on preparation for a movement for the riders.

Time: Keep the exercise in walk for 5–10 minutes unless the riders have warmed up prior to the lesson (in which case the warm-up can be shorter). Then commence the same exercise in trot for another 10 minutes or until improvement is seen.

On completion of the halt exercise, ask the ride to walk and give them a rest for a few minutes (walk on long rein). Then ask the ride to form a line across the centre line to explain the next exercise.

Check there is at least one horse's distance between riders.

Look for correct flexion and bend around the rider's inside leg on the circle.

ABC Logo

Explanation: This exercise will be ridden independently in trot. The instructor will have placed four cones, two either side of the centre line where the logo crosses it to allow for the riders to ride accurately.

The ride will commence large on the right rein at walk. When the instructor sees all riders are straight, the instructor commands 'ride prepare to trot, ride trot now and at A ride into three serpentine loops'. Upon reaching C they ride three serpentine loops back again towards A thus making up the ABC logo.

The riders need to watch for each other before crossing the centre line and make adjustments by either trotting on the spot to let another rider through first or riding a slightly longer trot to get through first. This trains the riders not only to work with their own horses, but also to watch for others.

Explain that if a rider's horse is not bending correctly around a circle, the rider should stay on that circle until achieving it and then recommence the exercise.

NB: The riders need to understand they are running the exercise themselves and that there is no set number of times each rider has to ride the half circle in the middle or the end circles. (i.e. can be half or twice or as often as needed).

Demonstration: Draw in the sand/ground the accurate shape of loops and show where the riders need to watch for each other and adjust their trot if needed.

Execution: Again, nominate a leader and ask the ride to ride forward to the large arena track and track right. Once all riders are travelling large in walk, begin to watch each rider's position and individually correct them before commencing the exercise. When the ride is moving correctly with safe distances, the instructor can commence the exercise in walk to check that the riders understood the explanation. The instructor may then prepare the ride to trot and trot on.

Aim: Look for smooth transitions from one rein to the other. With preparation, the rider will come from the right rein with the horse flexed and bent right, momentarily straighten whilst crossing the centre line, then flex and bend to the left without loss of rhythm.

The instructor should check and correct each rider's position.

If there are horses in the way as the riders are about to cross the centre line, help the riders to shorten or lengthen the stride without loss of rhythm by making sure they are observing and preparing early enough.

Time: This part of the exercise can be run for 20 minutes or until the instructor sees improvement in the riders. Make sure this includes a change of rein for the ride. The instructor may then give riders a long-rein walk break via the command 'ride, prepare to walk. Ride, walk now. Upon reaching C go large on the left rein on a long rein'.

Re-execution: After a few minutes break ask the riders to commence the same exercise on the left rein with the end 20-metre circles to be ridden in canter and the middle circle to be ridden in trot.

Aim: Look for smooth, calm transitions into and out of trot and canter with the rider combining flexion and bend in the transitions.

Time: This part of the exercise will also be run for 20 minutes. Be aware of the horse and rider fitness. If they are not fit things may start to go wrong as the combinations tire. The instructor may have to make the exercise easier by not demanding canter on the centre line but allowing the ride to pick up canter somewhere on the end circles and trot before the centre line.

Allow 10 minutes for each rein. Once improvement is seen, command the ride to walk, go large on the right rein and give the horses a long rein and a pat. Allow the ride a few minutes walk on long reins and ask them to form a ride on the centre line facing you.

Confirmation: Speak individually to the ride to comment positively on how they each performed in the lesson. Also make observations and give suggestions for improvement. Be specific and offer exercises which will give the rider direction.

End with positive reinforcement so the riders feel confident about training by themselves.

Glossary of terms

The following terms may appear in the exercise INSTRUCTIONS:

'The ride'	refers to the group of students, i.e. *'Ride prepare to trot'* means all riders prepare to trot
'Individually'	don't follow anyone else
'Go large'	follow the track around the edge of the whole arena
'Right rein'	the ride travels around the arena with their right side closest to the middle of the arena
'Left rein'	the ride travels around the arena with their left side closest to the middle of the arena
'Prepare to…'	the rider is expected to prepare the horse for the next move
'Change the rein'	means the ride will move from one direction to the other (e.g. left to right rein) on command from the instructor
'Single file'	the horses and riders ride nose to tail around the arena with one horses distance between them
'Open order'	the horses and riders ride nose to tail around the arena with three horses distance between them
'Gait'	specific order of footfall of the horse meaning walk, trot or canter
'Aid'	a physical and mental signal used by a rider to communicate a desired reaction from the horse
'Collection'	engagement of power in any gait, which is not the shortening of the gait but an elevation due to the increased energy coming from the engagement of the hindquarters
'Straight'	when the horse's spine is aligned with the track it is travelling whether it is straight or curved
'Rhythm'	correct sequence of footfalls in the regular beat of each gait
'Transition'	change of gait, or length of stride within a gait
'Flexion'	suppleness occurring at the poll either laterally (sideways) or?longitudinally (on the bit)
'Bend'	lateral – spine is uniformly curved from the poll to the tail (e.g. around a circle line)

'Bend'	lateral – spine is uniformly curved from the poll to the tail (e.g. around a circle line)
	longitudinal – the spine is stretched from the poll towards the ground allowing the stretch to reach the tail
'Half halt'	preparation for the halt in order to increase the activity of the hindquarters. This may be performed in any gait
'Leg yield'	lateral movement in which the horse moves forward and sideways whilst remaining straight and flexed away from the direction of movement
'Simple change'	a change of the canter lead where the horse is asked to walk and, after three to five steps, is asked to canter with the other leg leading
'Shoulder-in'	a collected lateral movement where the horse is asked to bring his shoulders in off the track whilst driving forward with his hindquarters thus creating three tracks in the movement. The horse is bent around the rider's inside leg and is flexed away from the direction of travel
'Travers'	another collected lateral movement where the horse is asked to bring its hindquarters in off the track around the rider's inside leg. The forehand remains on the original track so the horse is looking in the direction of travel

The following terms may appear in the exercise AIMS:

Safety	means to teach safety when riding in a group
Awareness	means to create appreciation of other riders
Halts	means to improve the halt transition
Straightness	means to improve straightness
Transitions	means to improve the accuracy and quality of transitions
Rhythm	means to improve the tempo of the horse's pace
Flexion & Bend	means to improve flexion and bend of the horse
Balance	means to improve the stability of the horse
Preparation	means to improve the rider's ability to plan ahead

Notes

Long and Short Reins

Warm-up exercise

gait	**Walk, Trot**
difficulty	**Ü**
no. of riders	**6+**

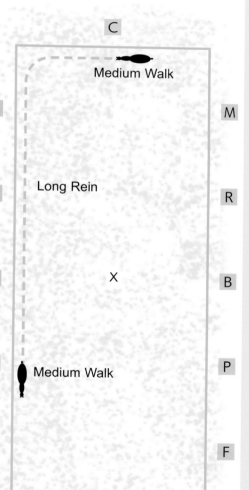

AIMS:

Transitions

INSTRUCTIONS:

At a letter ride the horse forward to a medium walk and as the rider passes a second letter allow the horse to stretch to a long-rein walk.

Passing the fourth letter the rider should ride forward to medium walk again.

Continue exercise until commanded further.

NOTES:

Riders should be working on a consistent rhythm whilst going from long rein to medium and return.

If the exercise is too difficult, give the riders more time in the long-rein walk to prepare themselves and the horse for medium walk.

Notes

Warm-up exercise

gait	**Walk, Trot**
difficulty	Ʊ
no. of riders	**6 +**

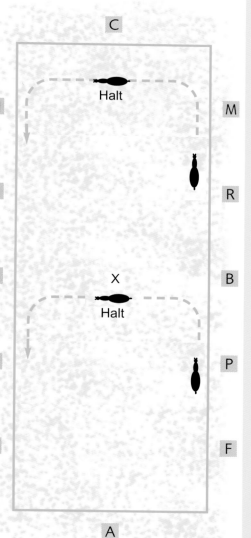

AIMS:

Awareness

Safety

Halts

Straightness

To improve accuracy of turns

INSTRUCTIONS:

All riders are trotting large (or walking depending on level) and when everyone is on the long side, the riders individually decide to turn across the arena and halt for four seconds across the centre line.

Walk or trot on when there is a space for the rider to merge into the long side on the same rein.

NOTES:

Riders must make accurate turns straight onto and away from their lines across the arena.

Notes

Halt across CL with Rein-back

Warm-up exercise

gait	**Walk, Trot, Canter**
difficulty	♘♘
no. of riders	**6 +**

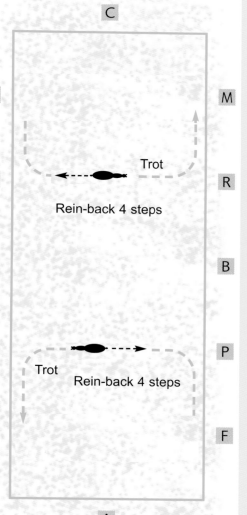

AIMS:

Awareness

Halts

To improve straight rein-back

To ride an accurate number of rein-back steps

INSTRUCTIONS:

When it is safe to do so, individually turn across the arena and halt across the centre line for four seconds.

Rein-back for one to four steps (depending on level of horse and rider).

Trot on when there is a space available. Upon reaching the track, continue on the same rein.

NOTES:

Check straightness first in the halt before the rein-back. Look straight ahead to help with straightness. Check spacing before trotting on.

The exercise can be ridden in canter (once warmed up) for the more experienced rider with a transition to walk then halt across the centre line. Riders may then continue in canter.

Notes

Warm-up exercise

gait	**Halt, Trot**
difficulty	♘
no. of riders	**6 +**

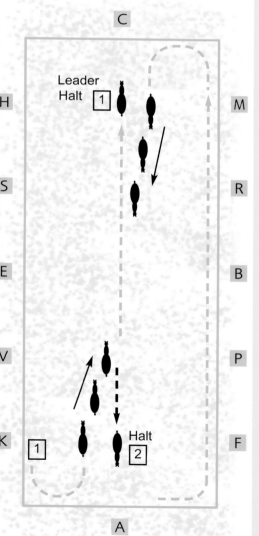

AIMS:

Halts

Straightness

INSTRUCTIONS:

With the ride going large on the left rein, the lead rider turns down the centre line at A.

The leader halts on the centre line facing C at the letter G and waits until the rear of the ride passes on the outside track. The rider then rejoins the rear of the ride and goes large.

Meanwhile, the second rider (as the new leader) has commenced the same exercise starting from C and halts at D at the opposite end. The exercise continues until all riders have been the leader and halted.

NOTES:

The rider turning down the centre line must turn *inside* the halted rider and move his/her horse across to the centre line in preparation for a straight halt.

Notes

Half 10-metre Circle to CL and Halt

Warm-up exercise

gait	**Halt, Trot**
difficulty	♘♘
no. of riders	**2–6**

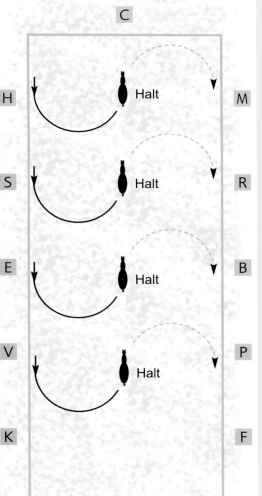

AIMS:

Halts

To improve accuracy of half 10-metre circles

INSTRUCTIONS:

On command ride half circle to centre line and halt.

On command half circle on same rein (i.e. 10-metre circle) or change the rein as shown.

Repeat exercise until instructor is satisfied with transitions.

NOTES:

The exercise may be done in walk, trot (for a warm-up) or canter according to levels.

The ride must be in 'closed' order because this exercise is ridden up and down the centre line and the long sides only.

Notes

Half 10-metre Circle and Walk

Warm-up exercise

gait	**Walk, Trot**
difficulty	Ʊ
no. of riders	**6 +**

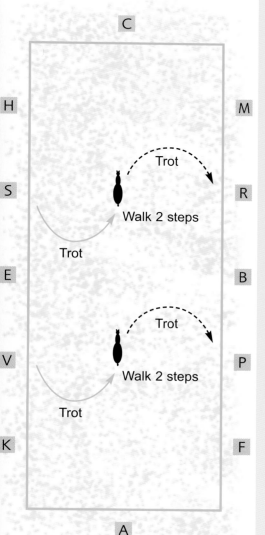

AIMS:

Transitions

Awareness

To improve half 10-metre circles

INSTRUCTIONS:

Individually ride a half 10-metre circle onto and away from the centre line.

At the centre line they walk straight down the centre line for two steps then trot on and half circle to either side when there is a space.

NOTES:

Keep riders tracking onto the centre line travelling in the same direction, e.g. from C facing A.

Notes

Warm-up exercise

gait	**Walk, Trot**
difficulty	**Ʊ**
no. of riders	**6 +**

C

Trot   Walk

H   M

S   R

Trot

E   Walk   X   Walk   B

Trot

V   P

K   F

Walk   Trot

A

AIMS:

To train and introduce the feel of the half halt

INSTRUCTIONS:

Ride trots large. When riders reach B, C, E or A, they ride forward to walk for five steps and then trot on again.

Once all riders have smooth transitions the instructor commands to decrease the number of walk strides to four strides, then three then two and one.

Ask the riders to set their horse up for walk and then change their mind and trot on thus riding a half halt.

NOTES:

Instructor counts aloud to each rider to check they can count the walk strides correctly.

Notes

Warm-up exercise

gait	**Walk, Trot**
difficulty	**Ʊ**
no. of riders	**6 +**

AIMS:

Transitions

Rhythm

INSTRUCTIONS:

At a letter walk.

At the next letter trot.

Change gait at every letter.

NOTES:

Watch riders are pushing their horse forward into smooth transitions.

If they need more time to prepare for changes, alter the exercise to make the change at every second letter.

C

Walk

Trot

H   M

Walk

S   R

Trot   X   B

E

V   Walk   P

K   F

A

Notes

Change Rein with New Leader

Warm-up exercise

gait	**Trot**
difficulty	�''☐
no. of riders	**6 +**

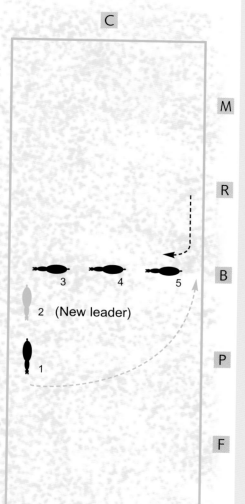

AIMS:

Preparation

INSTRUCTIONS:

The instructor describes this exercise then allows the riders to carry it out by themselves.

With 'Susan' leading, go large and change the rein any way you like. On completion, Susan half-circles to the rear of the ride and the second rider becomes the NEW leader.

The NEW leader changes the rein a different way.

The instructor supervises ensuring the leader half circles safely to allow for the new leader to continue the exercise.

NOTES:

This exercise continues until all riders have had a turn being leader and changing the rein in a different way from the previous rider.

Make sure the 'inventive' riders still ride a rhythmical, safe change of rein.

Notes

Beginner Snowman

gait	**Walk, Trot**
difficulty	♘
no. of riders	**2–6**

AIMS:

Transitions

Accuracy

Flexion and bend

Awareness

INSTRUCTIONS:

Set out snowman with cones. At A make a 20-metre circle for the body and at X make a 10-metre circle for the head as shown.

For younger riders, make a face on the snowman, e.g. leadrope for his smile and so forth.

NOTES:

Demonstrate the snowman track showing its correct size and direction for the 20-metre body (left rein) and 10-metre face (right rein). Change rein at snowman's neck!

Riders must be aware of each other.

Collisions at the neck may be avoided by either shortening or lengthening the trot or making the snowman's head a little larger.

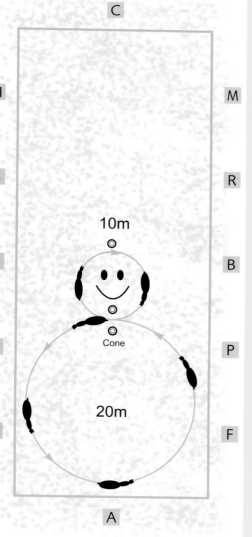

Notes

Double Transition Snowman

gait	**Walk, Trot**
difficulty	♘
no. of riders	**2–6**

AIMS:

Transitions

Accuracy

Awareness

Flexion and bend

INSTRUCTIONS:

At C or A ride onto the left-rein snowman.

After riding around his head, just before his neck, ride into walk for four steps (or halt for four seconds if there are only a few riders) then proceed into trot.

NOTES:

Riders must be aware of each other.

They may have to trot the neck, if the following rider is too close.

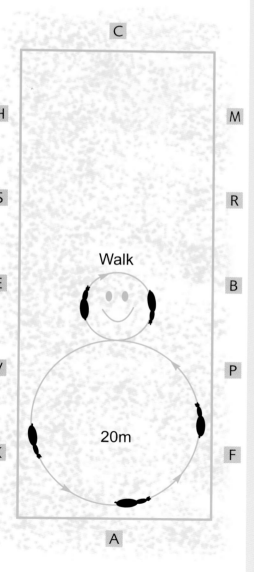

Notes

Canter Snowman

gait	**Trot, Canter**
difficulty	♘ ♘
no. of riders	**2–6**

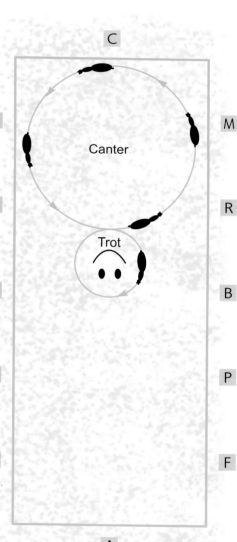

AIMS:

Improve transitions

Accuracy

Awareness

Flexion and bend

INSTRUCTIONS:

At C ride onto a left-rein snowman.

Once the snowman is accurate in trot, the ride can commence the exercise.

NOTES:

Whilst trotting around the snowman's head, rider prepares for canter transition as he approaches the neck. The rider changes flexion and bend and gives the aid for canter.

Rider completes a full 20-metre circle of the snowman's body in canter.

When approaching the neck, the rider prepares for trot changing flexion and bend and trots around the head.

Notes

gait	**Walk, Trot**
difficulty	Ŭ
no. of riders	**6 +**

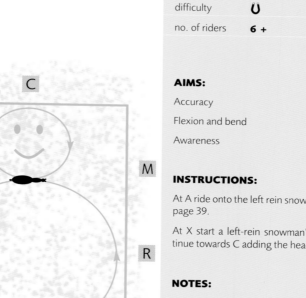

AIMS:

Accuracy

Flexion and bend

Awareness

INSTRUCTIONS:

At A ride onto the left rein snowman as shown on page 39.

At X start a left-rein snowman's body and continue towards C adding the head at the top.

NOTES:

The riders must check the opposite circle as they approach X and the snowman's neck so they cross in single file.

Use cones to help with the accuracy of the circles.

Riders may choose to ride half or 1½ heads to move from one snowman to the next.

Notes

Head-to-Head Snowman

gait	**Walk, Trot, Canter**
difficulty	♘ ♘
no. of riders	**6 +**

AIMS:

Awareness

Flexion and bend

Rhythm

INSTRUCTIONS:

At C ride onto left-rein snowman as shown. At X ride onto a left snowman's head towards A.

Complete the snowman and on returning to X ride onto a right snowman's head back towards C.

NOTES:

Depending on level, ride may trot 20-metre circles and walk 10-metre circles OR trot 10-metre circles and canter 20-metre circles.

Riders may ride half 10-metre circles (snowman's heads) OR 1½ 10-metre circles to give the rider more time to change flexion and bend.

Notes

gait	**Trot**
difficulty	♘
no. of riders	**2–6**

AIMS:

Awareness

Flexion and bend

Rhythm

Corners

INSTRUCTIONS:

At X ride onto a right squareman's head. On reaching his neck ride onto a left 20-metre square.

NOTES:

Riders have to prepare for the corners before arriving at them to keep their horses balanced.

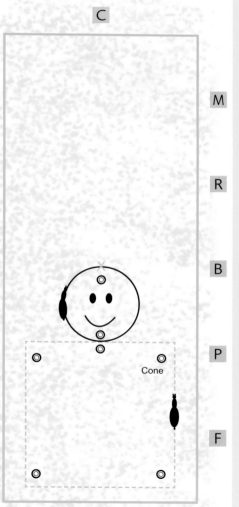

Notes

Monkey Ears

gait	**Walk, Trot**
difficulty	♘♘
no. of riders	**2–6**

AIMS:

Awareness

Rhythm

Flexion and bend changes

INSTRUCTIONS:

At E ride a 20-metre circle to the right and on crossing the centre line, ride onto a 10-metre circle on the opposite rein to form the monkey's ear. Repeat on the opposite side to form the other ear.

NOTES:

Riders should work on a consistent rhythm while changing from one circle to another.

If there are too many riders on a monkey's ear, riders may 'miss an ear' and continue on the face to ride the ear at the other side.

Beginners may ride trot on the face and walk around the ears.

Novice riders may rise trot the face and sit trot the ears.

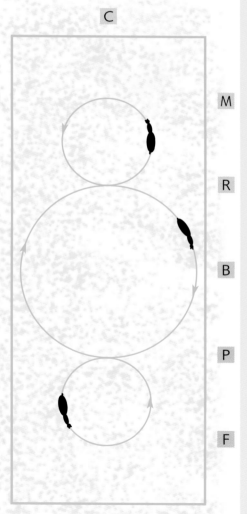

Notes

gait	**Walk, Trot**
difficulty	◡◡
no. of riders	**2–6**

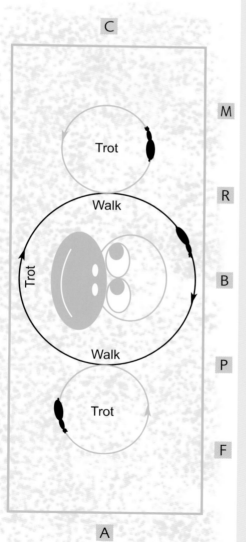

AIMS:

Awareness

Rhythm

Accurate transitions

Improve changes of flexion and bend

INSTRUCTIONS:

Ride the monkey's face from B or E.

On completion of a monkey ear, ride forward to walk for four steps and trot on again.

NOTES:

Riders must assess whether they are too close to each other for the walk transition.

A rider may have to omit a transition or an 'ear' to create more space.

Notes

Canter Monkey Ears

gait	**Trot, Canter**
difficulty	ŮŮ
no. of riders	**2–6**

AIMS:

Accurate transitions

Awareness

Rhythm

Improve changes of flexion and bend

INSTRUCTIONS:

On completion of a monkey ear, canter the 20-metre circle of the face. Prepare and then ride forwards to trot upon reaching the next ear.

NOTES:

Rider must be prepared for trot to achieve a balanced, rhythmic transition and then change flexion and bend for the new circle.

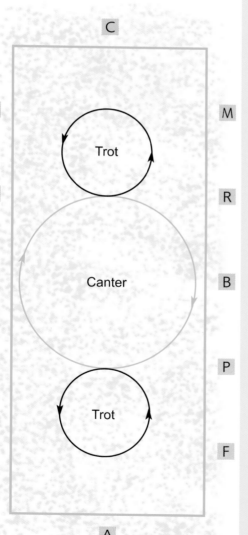

Notes

Counter Canter Monkey Ears

gait	**Canter**
difficulty	♘♘♘
no. of riders	**2–3**

AIMS:

Awareness

Rhythm

Flexion and bend

Balance

INSTRUCTIONS:

On reaching an ear, ride true canter and when balanced, canter onto the face.

Counter canter to the opposite ear and complete the ear in true canter.

NOTES:

An educated horse will manage the full circle in a balanced rhythmic canter.

A less educated horse should manage the half circle and be able to rebalance on the smaller circle.

If the rider has trouble achieving counter canter allow him/her to make a shallow half circle e.g. not all the way to E or B.

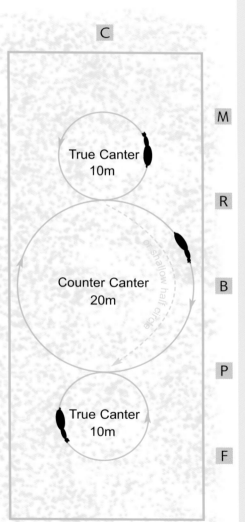

Notes

gait	**Trot**
difficulty	♘♘
no. of riders	**6 +**

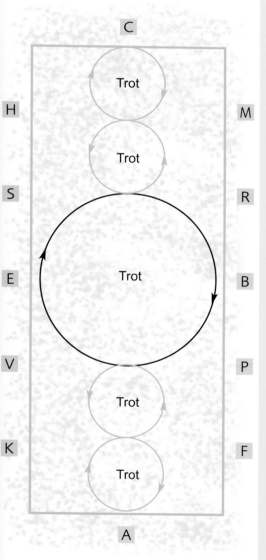

AIMS:

Safety

Awareness

Balance

Flexion and bend

INSTRUCTIONS:

At E ride onto right-rein monkey face then double monkey ears (or monkey ear and earring).

NOTES:

If there are too many riders on one ear, riders should omit an ear or ride one ear twice to allow each other more space.

Notes

Double Canter Monkey Ears

gait	**Trot, Canter**
difficulty	◡◡◡
no. of riders	**6 +**

AIMS:

Safety

Awareness

Flexion and bend

INSTRUCTIONS:

At E ride onto the double monkey ear pattern. Canter on the face (20-metre circle).

Trot the first ear and canter the second. Or trot for both ears for novice horses.

NOTES:

More advanced horses may canter all circles with a simple change on the centre line.

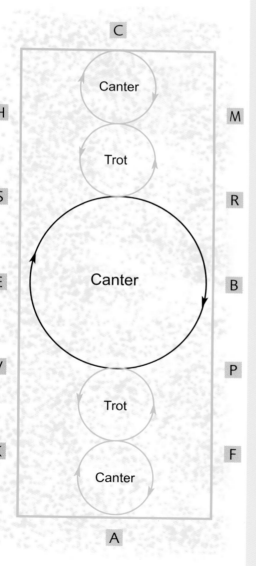

Notes

gait	**Trot**
difficulty	**ÜÜÜ**
no. of riders	**6 +**

AIMS:

Safety

Awareness

Lateral work

Balance

INSTRUCTIONS:

Individually trot a right-rein monkey ear into double ears.

The ride may choose to ride large from the face into a shoulder-in down one long side, then join the earring or continue large to ride travers on the other side.

The riders then rejoin the face.

NOTES:

The lateral work can be ridden at both ends of the arena according to their level of training.

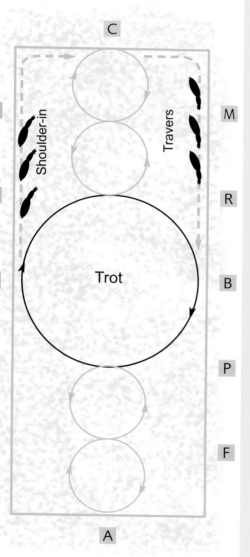

Notes

Canter Circles and Trot Large

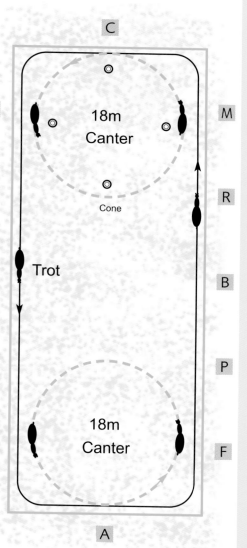

gait	**Trot, Canter**
difficulty	♡
no. of riders	**6 +**

AIMS:

Awareness

Transitions

To improve planning and preparation

INSTRUCTIONS:

At A and C canter onto an 18-metre circle. Upon completion trot and ride large to the next circle.

NOTES:

Depending on rider level, the circles may be 15 metres or 10 metres in diameter.

Use cones to mark circles.

Notes

Canter Circles and Extended Trot

gait	**Trot, Canter**
difficulty	♞♞
no. of riders	**6 +**

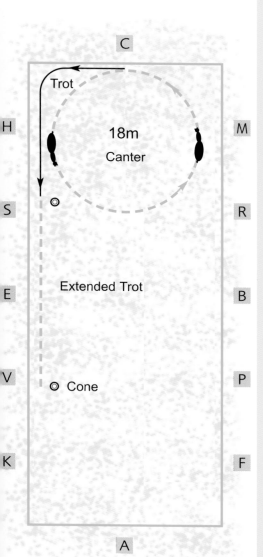

AIMS:

Awareness

Transitions

Rhythm in trot and canter

INSTRUCTIONS:

Set up pattern as shown on page 65.

Leave the circle at C at ride forward to trot. At S lengthen the trot.

At V push forward to working trot.

Enter the circle at A in canter and repeat the exercise between P and R.

NOTES:

Use cones to mark extended trot points.

Only half of this exercise has been illustrated.

Notes

gait	**Walk, Trot, Canter**
difficulty	U
no. of riders	**6 +**

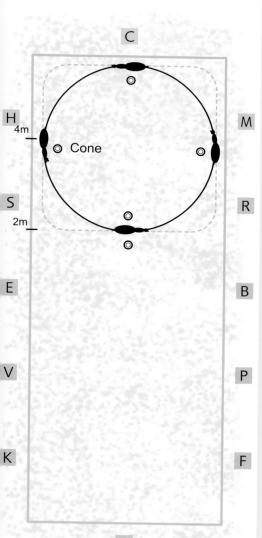

AIMS:

Accuracy

Rhythm

INSTRUCTIONS:

From C ride onto a 20-metre circle, i.e. from C the tangent points are C, four metres past H, two metres past R and S on the centre line and four metres before M.

(See illustration.)

When all riders are riding accurately around the circle, ask them to ride onto a 20-metre square.

NOTES:

The instructor may have to put cones out to hold the accuracy.

If the instructor wants the ride to ride large, the circle can remain at C whilst the square is placed at A.

This exercise may also be ridden at canter.

Notes

Canter Half 20-metre Circles

gait	**Trot, Canter**
difficulty	**Ʊ**
no. of riders	**6 +**

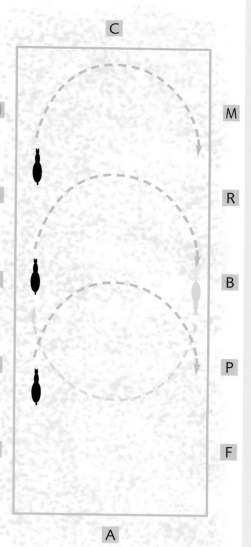

AIMS:

Awareness

Accuracy

Transitions

INSTRUCTIONS:

The ride trots large and when it is safe to do so, riders leave the track and canter a half 20-metre circle across the arena until they reach the other side where they return to trot.

NOTES:

Look up and about for a space.

Riders canter as they leave the track, ride an accurate half 20-metre circle and trot upon returning to the track.

Riders may depart from either side of the arena provided it is safe to do so. They must be aware of other riders on the opposite side.

Notes

Half 20-metre Circles Trot to Canter

gait	**Trot, Canter**
difficulty	♘♘
no. of riders	**2–6**

AIMS:

Awareness

To improve the trot-canter and canter-trot transitions

To improve both gaits

To improve balance

INSTRUCTIONS:

At C ride a full 20-metre circle in trot. Crossing the centre line, canter a half 20-metre circle back to C.

Repeat the exercise then go large to the other end and start again at A.

NOTES:

Riders need to prepare for transitions and be aware of other riders.

Only half of this exercise is illustrated.

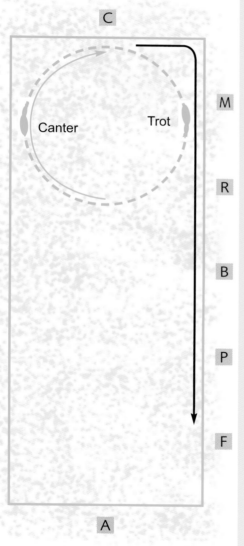

Notes

Walk, Trot, Canter Circles

gait	**Walk, Trot, Canter**
difficulty	ÜÜ
no. of riders	**2–6**

AIMS:

To improve the upward and downward transitions

INSTRUCTIONS:

Commence the exercise on the right rein.

At A walk and ride onto an 18-metre circle.

The first quarter of the circle is ridden in walk. Then half circle trot followed by quarter circle canter.

At K trot and go large.

Repeat the exercise upon reaching H. At M trot and go large.

Lenghten trot between R–P and V–S letters.

NOTES:

Exercise is run at both A and C circles.

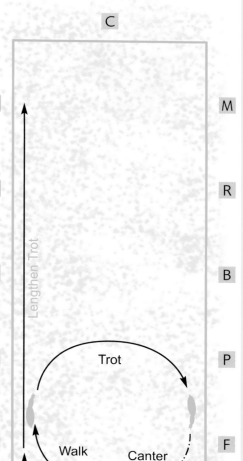

Notes

Chopsticks Exercise

gait	**Walk, Trot, Canter**
difficulty	♘♘
no. of riders	**6 +**

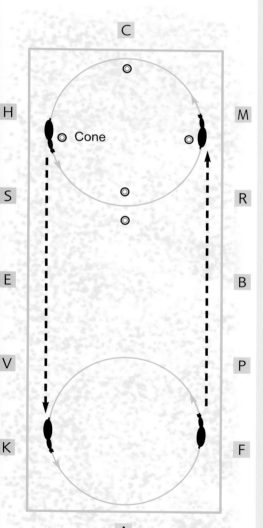

AIMS:

To create awareness of hands

To create a quiet, still rein aid

INSTRUCTIONS:

Ride onto an 18-metre circle with chopsticks underneath the thumbs.

NOTES:

Riders carry chopsticks (or small whips) under their thumbs.

Have the leader in control riding without chopsticks, if required.

Steering may be a problem, so create an easy exercise, e.g. 18-metre circles at A and C and go large proceeding from one to the other.

Notes

gait	**Trot, Canter**
difficulty	♘♘
no. of riders	**2–6**

AIMS:

To improve horse's balance

To improve rider's co-ordination

INSTRUCTIONS:

At C and A ride a full 20-metre circle.

Decrease the size of the circle to between 10 and 15 metres in diameter.

On completion of a full small circle leg yield back to the 20-metre circle. Go large and repeat the exercise at the opposite end of the arena.

NOTES:

The smaller circle is 10–15 metres in diameter depending on the education of the horses and riders.

The more educated the horse, the smaller the circle.

Always complete full circles before changing the diameter. This helps to keep the exercise flowing.

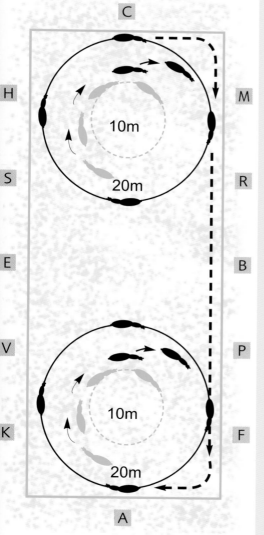

Notes

gait	**Halt, Trot, Canter**
difficulty	**UU**
no. of riders	**2–6**

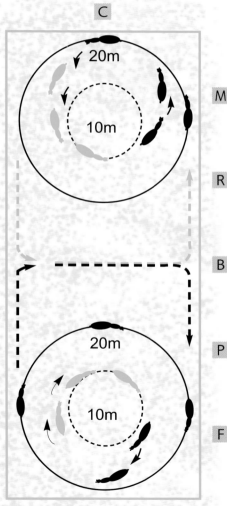

AIMS:

Balance

Transitions

Awareness

INSTRUCTIONS:

At C ride a left 20-metre circle.

Decrease the size of the circle to 10 metres in diameter and leg yield out.

Between E and B turn across the centre line.

At B track right and at A ride a right 20-metre circle.

Decrease the size of the circle to 10 metres in diameter and leg yield out.

NOTES:

The riders must ride a straight line across the arena from E to B.

Always complete full circles before changing the diameter.

Riders need to be aware of each other approaching from the opposite direction at E.

Notes

gait	**Walk, Canter**
difficulty	Ư
no. of riders	**2–6**

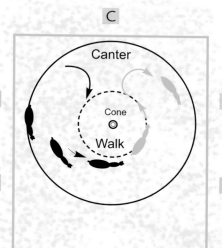

AIMS:

To improve the canter whilst being in control of the ride

Approaching walk to canter and canter to walk transitions

INSTRUCTIONS:

At A or C ride a 20-metre circle.

The ride decreases their circle to 10 metres in the middle of this circle. Upon reaching the 10-metre circle, the riders walk with their horses nose to tail around it.

On command the riders individually outwards half circle and canter as they depart the 10-metre circle, onto the 20-metre circle.

After cantering twice around the 20-metre circle as the rider begins to pass the rider who was in front of him/her on the 10-metre circle, he/she prepares to turn via an inward half circle back into his/her original space and walk.

NOTES:

For a large group use the A and the C 20-metre circles. Divide the group into no more than five riders per circle then decrease both circles to 10 metres. (If in trot, forward to walk upon reaching the 10-metre circle).

Beginners should make transitions in to and out of canter via trot.

Notes

gait	**Walk, Trot, Canter**
difficulty	U
no. of riders	6 +

AIMS:

Accuracy

Awareness

INSTRUCTIONS:

From the front, number off in twos (i.e. one, two, one, two etc).

At E (or B) turn to X

At X number one's ride a 20-metre circle left rein and number two's ride a 20-metre circle right rein.

NOTES:

This exercise is ridden in open order to allow for transitions to be added.

There should only ever be one rider at a time over X.

Change rein regularly from one circle to the next by naming a leader on each circle.

Ask the leaders to change rein from their circle through X onto the opposite circle.

This exercise can be changed into snowmen (page 39) with their heads at A and C.

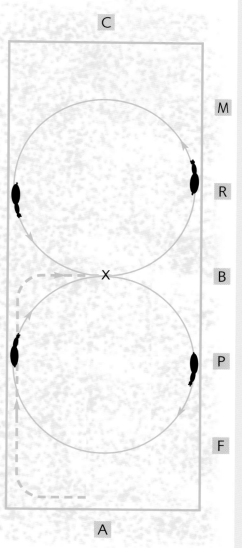

Notes

Bug Eyes

gait	**Trot**
difficulty	**U**
no. of riders	**2–6**

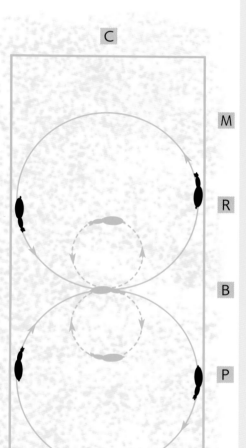

AIMS:

Awareness

Flexion and bend

Rhythm

INSTRUCTIONS:

At X ride a 20-metre circle onto the left rein followed by a 10-metre circle on the left rein.

Upon reaching X, change to the right rein and repeat.

NOTES:

All circles 10 metres or smaller should be ridden at sitting trot.

Riders need to be aware of each other. They may have to shorten the trot to allow another rider to cross X first.

Notes

gait	**Trot, Canter**
difficulty	ʊʊ
no. of riders	**2–6**

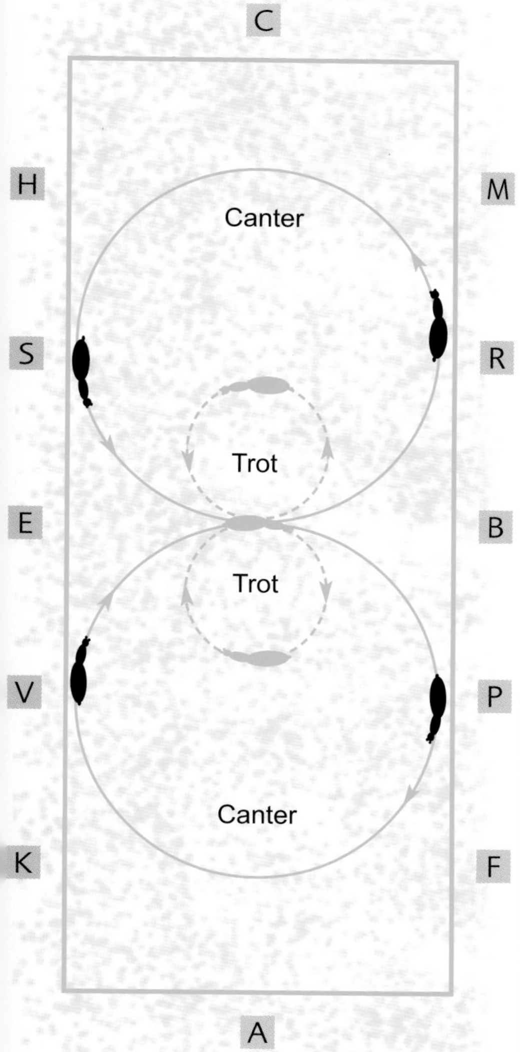

AIMS:

Flexion and bend

Rhythm

Transitions

INSTRUCTIONS:

At X canter a 20-metre circle on the left rein followed by a trot transition and ride a 10-metre circle on the left rein.

Next, canter a right rein 20-metre circle followed by a trot transition into a 10-metre circle on the right rein.

NOTES:

All circles 10 metres or smaller should be ridden at sitting trot.

Riders must watch for each other and may have to shorten the canter to allow another rider to cross X first.

C

H   M

Canter

S   R

Trot

E   B

Trot

V   P

Canter

K   F

A

Notes

gait	**Trot**
difficulty	♘
no. of riders	**6 +**

AIM:

Awareness

Flexion and bend

Rhythm

INSTRUCTIONS:

Ride onto a 3-loop serpentine from A.

Upon reaching C, ride a 3-loop serpentine back to A.

NOTES:

Riders must watch for each other so one rider at a time crosses the centre line.

Riders may have to shorten or lengthen the strides slightly to allow the exercise to flow.

Use cones to help with accuracy.

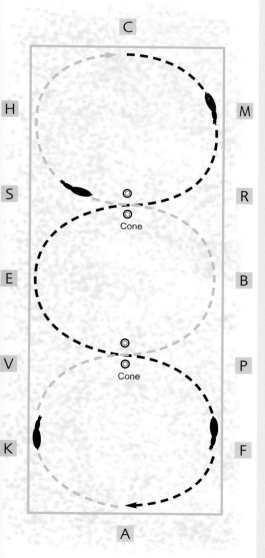

Notes

gait	**Trot**
difficulty	♘
no. of riders	**6 +**

AIM:

To improve the sitting trot

To work on change of flexion and bend

Awareness

INSTRUCTIONS:

Commence a 3-loop serpentine at C on the right rein and on the first crossing of the centre line enter a 10-metre circle in sitting trot on the same rein.

Continue the serpentine loop.

Ride another 10-metre circle at the second crossing of the centre line on the same rein.

Complete the serpentine loop then repeat the exercise from A to C.

NOTES:

Upon reaching the centre line after the 10-metre circle has been completed, the ride may walk for two strides, change flexion and bend and then trot on.

The 10-metre circles must be ridden in sitting trot.

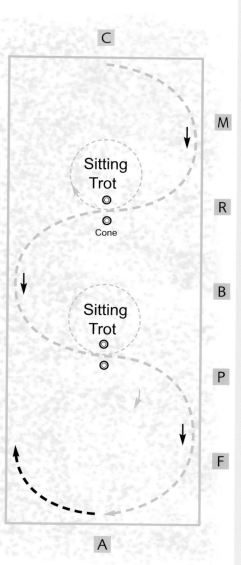

Notes

gait	**Trot**
difficulty	ŨŨ
no. of riders	**6 +**

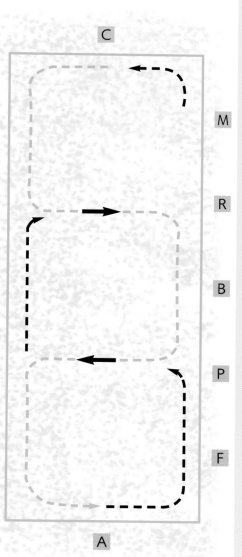

AIMS:

Awareness

Balance

Flexion and bend

INSTRUCTIONS:

On the left rein at A, commence a 3-loop square serpentine, working on balanced turns.

At C return to A in the same manner.

NOTES:

Riders must ride correct corners by preparing before arriving at the corner.

Notes

gait	**Trot, Canter**
difficulty	ՍՍՍ
no. of riders	**6 +**

AIM:

Awareness

Balance

Accuracy

To improve canter corners

INSTRUCTIONS:

At C ride into a 3-square serpentine in canter with a simple change on the centre line.

The exercise is completed by returning to C in the same manner.

NOTES:

Depending on level of riders, some may have to trot the middle square.

Preparation for the simple change is important so that riders can keep the corners of the serpentine accurate.

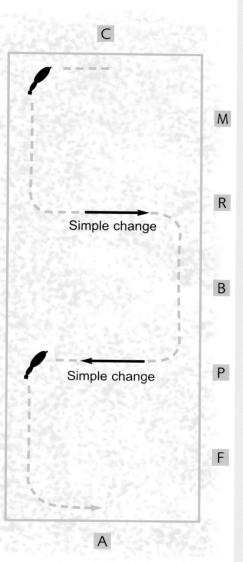

C

H

S

E

V

K

M

R

B

P

F

A

Simple change

Simple change

Notes

gait	**Trot**
difficulty	℧℧℧
no. of riders	**6 +**

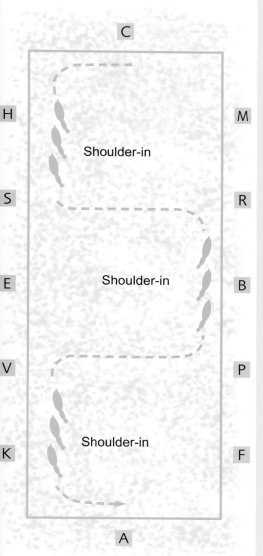

AIMS:

Awareness

To improve corners

To improve transitions into the shoulder-in

INSTRUCTIONS:

At C ride onto a 3-square serpentine to A.

Ride shoulder-in on the long sides.

Repeat the exercise from A to C.

NOTES:

Riders must ride correct corners.

The exercise may be changed by riding the middle loop as a half circle to become half square – half circle – half square thus riding shoulder-in on one rein only.

Notes

gait	**Trot**
difficulty	♘♘
no. of riders	**6 +**

AIMS:

Flexion and bend

Rhythm

INSTRUCTIONS:

At C ride onto a 6- or 8-loop serpentine.

Where the serpentine meets the outside track (long side) ride a small circle (7–8 metre diameter) then resume the serpentine.

NOTES:

If a rider has trouble on a certain circle, continue on the circle until the horse feels balanced.

To improve accuracy, use cones to mark the serpentine loops.

More serpentine loops will create smaller circles.

Notes

gait	**Walk, Trot, Canter**
difficulty	Ʊ
no. of riders	**6 +**

AIM:

To move the horse around the arena keeping the same rhythm

To improve balance

INSTRUCTIONS:

Ride two loops of between five and ten metres down the long side.

NOTES:

Position cones to improve accuracy.

Riders should be working on straightness and rhythm.

Advanced riders may lengthen the stride out towards the centre line and return to working trot back to the track.

For novice, position the cones close to arena sides to make the loops easier to reach.

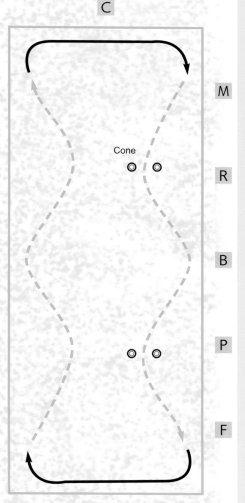

C

H   M

Cone

S   R

E   B

V   P

K   F

A

Notes

gait	**Walk**
difficulty	**Ü**
no. of riders	**6 +**

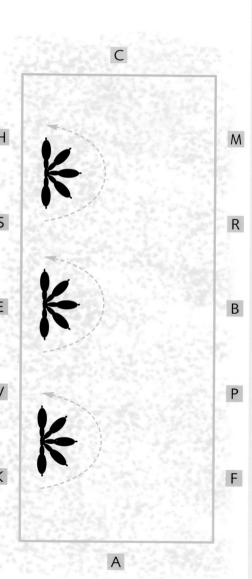

AIMS:

To teach the horse and rider the lateral aids

INSTRUCTIONS:

For turn on the forehand to the left.

Use your left leg behind the girth and have flexion slightly to the left so that the corner of the horse's left eye is visible to the rider.

Ask the horse to move sideways to the right and away from the pressure of the left leg whilst restraining and then releasing any forward movement with the seat and rein aids.

NOTES:

Riders begin on the right rein and line up in open order along a long side. The instructor may have to help each rider individually at first by placing the rider's leg behind the girth.

Once all riders can successfully achieve a turn on the forehand, the instructor can work the exercise as a group.

When asking for turn on the forehand, make sure the rider understands to ask the horse's hindquarters to turn towards the centre of the arena whilst marking time at the front.

Notes

gait	**Walk, Trot**
difficulty	℧℧
no. of riders	**2–6**

AIMS:

Awareness

Planning and preparation

To improve lateral aids

INSTRUCTIONS:

Ask the riders to begin to 'change the rein' across the diagonal in walk.

Prepare them for a turn on the forehand to the right either from halt or walk (collecting the steps first). Riders should see the right eye lash and use the right leg to turn.

Ask the ride to trot.

NOTES:

Across the diagonal, the turn on the forehand is ridden in the direction the ride came from.

For example: As shown in the diagram the ride came from the right rein. The turn on the forehand direction is determined by the way the horse is flexed.

On completion the ride has changed direction and trots on to the left rein (back in the direction they came from).

The instructor commands this exercise.

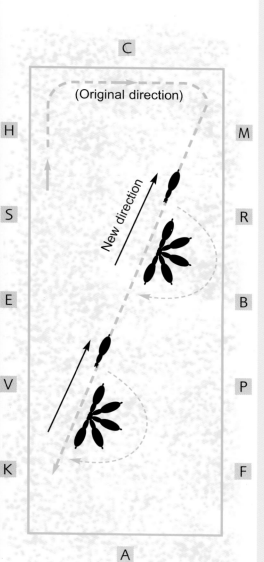

C

(Original direction)

H

M

New direction

S

R

E

B

V

P

K

F

A

Notes

Three-quarter Lines and Leg Yield

gait	**Walk, Trot, Canter**
difficulty	♘♘
no. of riders	**6 +**

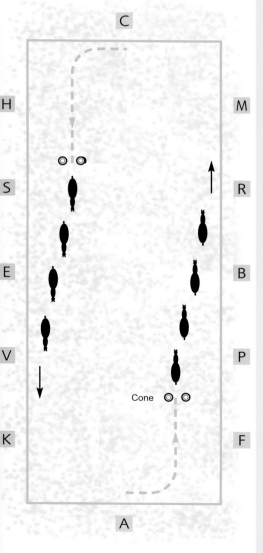

AIMS:

To improve lateral work

Rhythm

INSTRUCTIONS:

At three-quarter line after A from the right rein, the ride travels straight for five or six strides then leg yields to the right until the riders reach the track and go large.

Ride the same exercise upon reaching C.

NOTES:

To leg yield the rider asks the horse to move forward and sideways from his/her inside leg towards the outside rein until reaching the outside track.

The rider may see the inside eyelash only as the horse flexes away from the direction of travel.

Notes

Leg Yield and Half Circles

gait	**Walk, Trot**
difficulty	♘♘
no. of riders	**6 +**

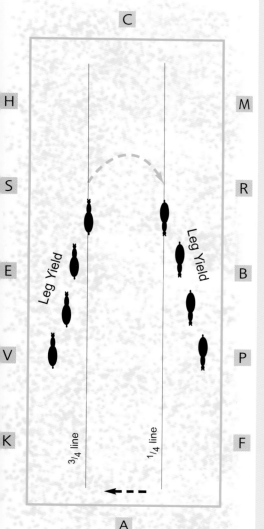

AIMS:

Awareness

Lateral aids

Rhythm

INSTRUCTIONS:

When it is safe to do so, leg yield to the three-quarter line and half circle to the opposite quarter line.

Then leg yield to the long side away from the centre line.

NOTES:

Riders must be accurate with quarter and three-quarter lines so the exercise flows for all riders.

If riders are not ready to leg yield into the quarter line, they may go large and turn down the three quarter line and leg yield to the large arena track.

Notes

gait	**Trot, Canter**
difficulty	♘♘
no. of riders	**6 +**

AIMS:

Awareness

Transitions

Accuracy

INSTRUCTIONS:

The ride canters along the short sides of the arena.

Upon reaching the long sides ride forward to trot.

Work on accurate transitions in the corners – into and out of canter.

NOTES:

Open order is better for this exercise.

If too close to the rider in front, riders may practise sitting trot instead of canter along the short sides.

A variation of this exercise is to include a half 20-metre circle in canter across the arena (page 71).

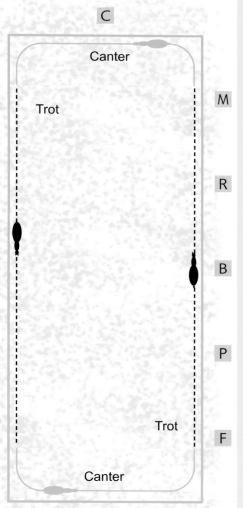

C

Canter

H

Trot

M

S

R

E

B

V

P

Trot

K

F

Canter

A

Notes

Canter Short Circles

gait	**Trot, Canter**
difficulty	ひひひ
no. of riders	**2–6**

AIMS:

Transitions

Rhythm

INSTRUCTIONS:

Canter the short sides of the arena and at C and A canter a 10-metre (or 15-metre) circle.

Trot upon returning to the long side.

NOTES:

The size of the canter circle will depend on the education of the horse and rider.

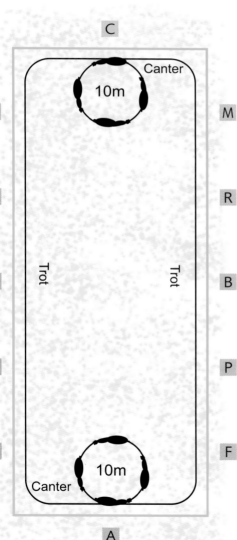

Notes

Lengthen and Shorten Canter

gait	**Canter**
difficulty	ᘮᘮ
no. of riders	**6 +**

AIMS:

Transitions

Rhythm

INSTRUCTIONS:

Between P and R and between S and V ride forward to a lengthened canter.

NOTES:

When starting this exercise give riders time to build the canter to a longer stride.

Once they have the feel then the instructor may demand accuracy in the transitions at the letters.

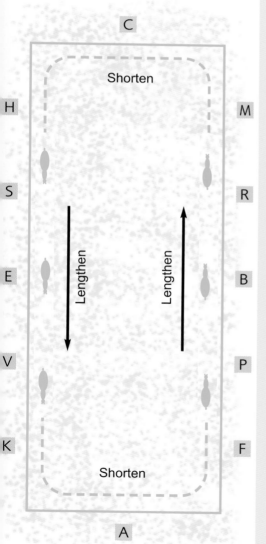

Notes

gait	**Walk, Trot, Canter**
difficulty	Ü
no. of riders	**6 +**

AIMS:

Straightness

Good turns

INSTRUCTIONS:

Place the cones as shown.

After C, the ride turns onto the three-quarter line.

Turn down the three-quarter line and ride straight between the cones.

The exercise can be performed in walk, trot or canter with transitions in between, i.e. canter down the three-quarter line. At H trot and canter upon reaching the large arena track.

The exercise may be downgraded to trot. Then walk at S and trot upon reaching V.

NOTES:

More advanced riders may trot at H and canter at V keeping the line straight.

Exercise may be conducted on both three-quarter lines.

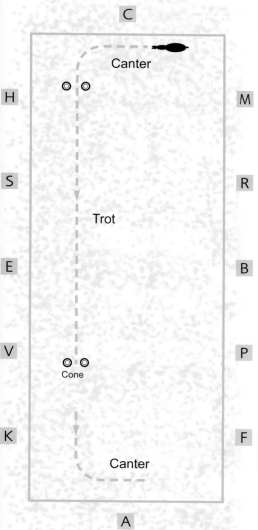

Notes

Halts on Straight Lines

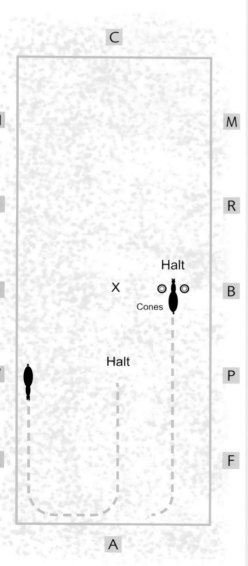

gait	Halt, Walk, Trot
difficulty	♘
no. of riders	6 +

AIMS:

Transitions

Awareness

INSTRUCTIONS:

The riders independently ride down the centre or three-quarter lines and halt at a point nominated by the instructor, e.g. a pair of cones.

The halt is held for five seconds.

Trot on.

Upon reaching the end of the arena, track onto the same rein and go large.

NOTES:

The transition must be forward and calm.

Riders should halt through the walk if their halts are abrupt.

Notes

gait	Halt, Trot, Canter
difficulty	ᴜᴜ
no. of riders	6 +

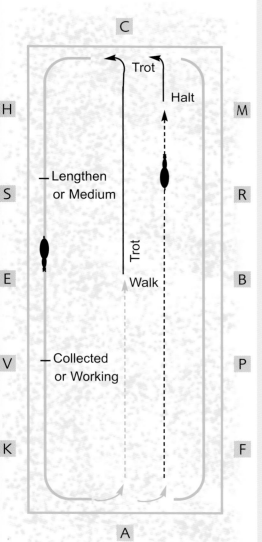

AIMS:

Awareness

Transitions

Halts

Straightness

INSTRUCTIONS:

The exercise is shown on the left rein. Riders ride independently and may use any or all of the straight line tracks.

1. SV on the outside track – Between the letters S and V on the outside track lengthen the strides.

2. Three-quarter line – Turn onto the three-quarter lines and halt between H and M for five seconds.

3. Centre line – Turn down the centre line from A to C and at X walk five steps.

4. Canter in the corner before F down?the long side and trot at M.

NOTES:

Riders should stay in halt until they see it is safe to go large.

The riders should use the exercise to work on straightness. Cones may be useful to mark the three-quarter lines.

Notes

Lateral Straight Line Tracks

gait	**Walk, Trot**
difficulty	∪∪∪
no. of riders	**6 +**

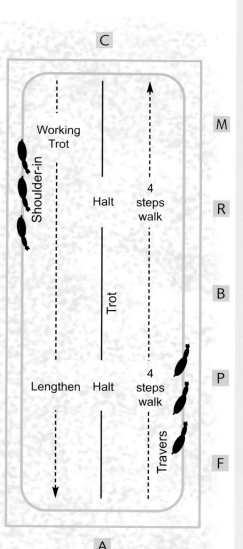

AIMS:

Awareness

Transitions

Balance

Preparation

INSTRUCTIONS:

This exercise is shown on the left rein. Riders ride independently and may use any or all of the straight line tracks.

1. Centre line – Halt at the R–S line and the V–P line.

2. Three-quarter line after A – Walk four steps at the P–V line and the R–S line.

3. Three-quarter line after C – Lengthen from the H–M to the V–P line.

4. H–E on the outside track – Shoulder-in.

5. F–B on the outside track – Travers or working trot.

NOTES:

Exercise can be changed as needed.

Easier exercises for newer riders (e.g. no lateral work).

Cones may be used as markers for the riders.

Notes

gait	**Walk, Trot**
difficulty	♘♘
no. of riders	**6 +**

AIMS:

Awareness

Transitions

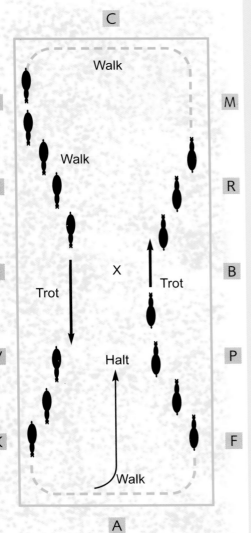

INSTRUCTIONS:

At C walk and at H leg yield to the quarter line or centre line.

Trot on again and leg yield back out to the track.

At A walk.

NOTES:

If there are many riders on one side, a rider may go large and miss the leg yield to gain more space.

The ride may also turn up the centre line from A to C and halt between the V–P, and the S–R markers. At C go large.

Notes

gait	**Trot**
difficulty	**U**
no. of riders	**6+**

AIMS:

Straightness

Rhythm

Accuracy

INSTRUCTIONS:

At C and A the ride individually rides onto a 15-metre circle.

After the corners the ride loops out towards X and return to the same side.

NOTES:

Place cones out to indicate depth of loops (i.e. lower level riders need not go out as far as X).

Mark out 15-metre (or 10-metre) circles with cones if needed, to prevent collisions between the circle and the loop riders.

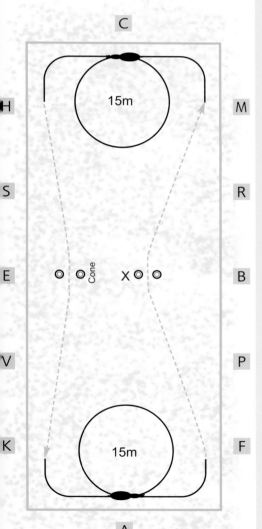

Notes

gait	**Canter**
difficulty	♘♘
no. of riders	**6 +**

AIMS:

Awareness

Rhythm

Accuracy

INSTRUCTIONS:

At C and A the ride canters individually onto an 18-metre circle.

From the corners they loop out towards X and return to the same side.

NOTES:

Place cones to indicate depth of loops. They may be anywhere between B and X (or E and X) remembering that less experienced combinations should only loop to five metres.

To make the exercise easier, the loops may be ridden in trot, cantering in the first corner then trotting in the second.

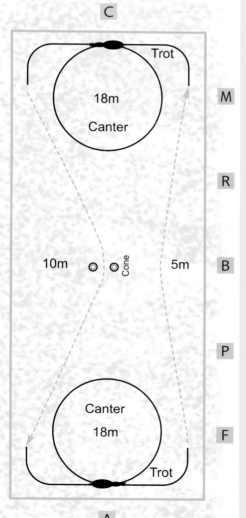

Notes

gait	**Trot**
difficulty	♘
no. of riders	**6 +**

AIMS:

Straightness

Rhythm

Accuracy

INSTRUCTIONS:

At C the ride trots onto a 15-metre circle.

From the corners the ride loops out toward X and return to the same side.

The ride then turns down the three-quarter line after A and leg yields to the track.

NOTES:

Place cones to indicate depth of the loops (i.e. lower level riders need not go out as far as X).

If needed mark the 15- or 10-metre circles with cones to prevent collisions with riders entering onto the loop.

Riders may have to ride a second circle to maintain separation from the rider in front.

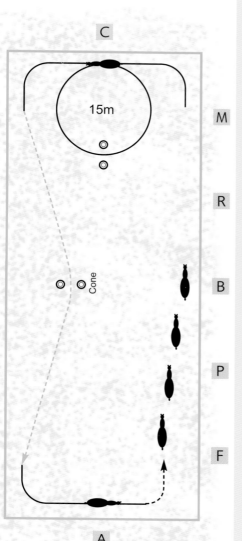

Notes

Looples

gait	**Halt, Trot**
difficulty	♘♘
no. of riders	**6 +**

AIM:

Awareness

Flexion and bend

Transitions

INSTRUCTIONS:

From H, on the left rein, the ride trots a loop of 9 metres towards X.

Upon reaching X the ride trots a 9-metre circle right and then continues out to K.

The straight diagonal sections of the loop may be ridden in the lengthened strides and then collected for the circles or the corners.

NOTES:

Riders may turn up the centre line from A to C only and ride a halt at the V–P and the R–S lines.

Place cones either side of X to allow a clear path for riding up the centre line to the halts.

Outward circles must be in sitting trot because they are smaller than 10 metres.

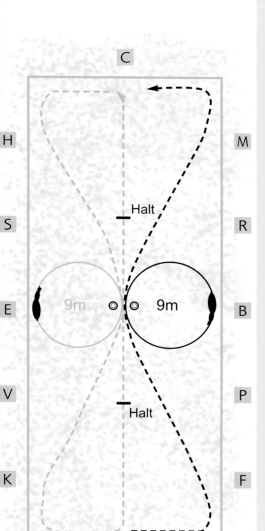

C

H

S

E   9m   9m

V

K

M

R

B

P

F

A

Halt

Halt

Notes

gait	**Walk, Trot**
difficulty	∪∪
no. of riders	**6 +**

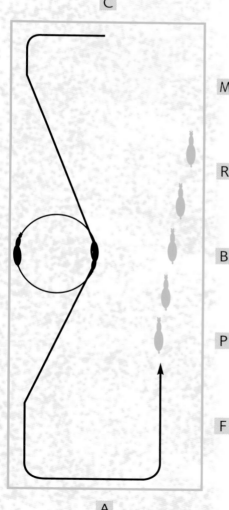

AIMS:

Awareness

Preparation

To improve changes of flexion and bend within the same rhythm

INSTRUCTIONS:

The ride turns down the three-quarter line after A and leg yields to the track.

After H the ride trots to X, changes flexion and bend for the 10-metre circle in the new direction towards E.

Upon reaching X again, the ride returns to the large arena track via a diagonal line toward K.

NOTES:

The 10-metre circle must be ridden in sitting trot.

The centre line and halt may also be added to this exercise.

Notes

gait	**Trot**
difficulty	**ŬŬ**
no. of riders	**6 +**

AIMS:

Awareness

Transitions

INSTRUCTIONS:

The ride individually trots a half 10-metre circle to the centre line then each rider straightens and lengthens on a diagonal line to the opposite side.

Each rider then rides forward to working trot upon reaching the large arena track.

NOTES:

Riders should work on transitions.

The riders must straighten before lengthening. Riders must be aware of others and only half-circle if there is room to lengthen to the other side.

This exercise must be run from one side only, i.e. enter the half-circles from the HEK side only to minimise the need to watch for others on the opposite side.

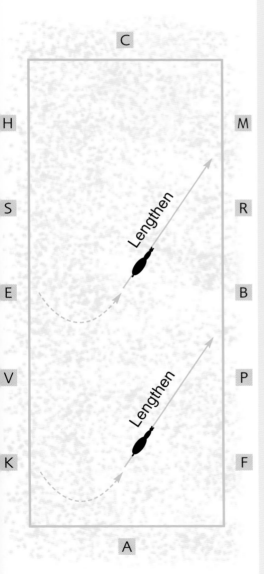

Notes

gait	**Walk, Trot**
difficulty	♘♘
no. of riders	**6 +**

AIM:

Awareness

Balance

Improve balance through a corner

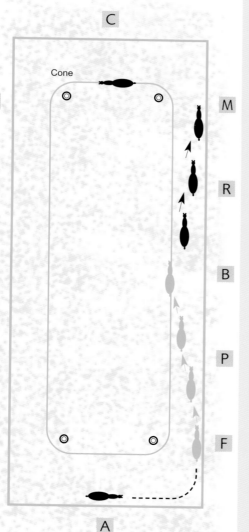

INSTRUCTIONS:

The riders individually decrease (leg yield) to the small rectangle and return (leg yield) to the large arena when there is a space available.

The riders may complete one small rectangle then leg yield back to the large arena track.

NOTES:

Riders must concentrate on riding the corners in both the small and large arenas.

Notes

gait	**Walk, Trot, Canter**
difficulty	ΟΟΟ
no. of riders	**6 +**

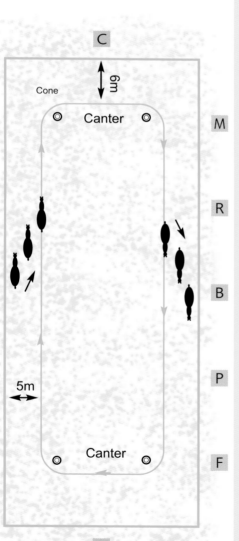

AIMS:

Awareness

Rhythm

Straightness

Transitions

INSTRUCTIONS:

The riders individually decrease (by leg yielding) to the smaller arena then canter once around the rectangle.

The riders then leg yield out and trot upon reaching the large arena.

NOTES:

Riders must be aware of each other.

Riders who have difficulty with the canter transition may canter in the corner of the small arena, leg yield out to the large arena then trot upon reaching the track.

Notes

Double Arena with Circles

gait	**Walk, Trot, Canter**
difficulty	℧℧℧
no. of riders	**6 +**

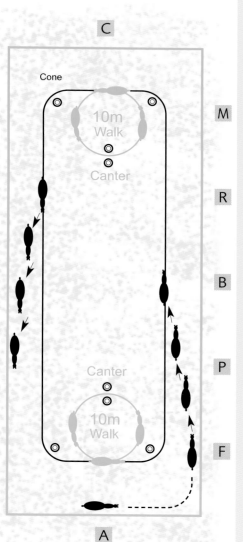

AIMS:

Awareness

Rhythm

Transitions

INSTRUCTIONS:

When commanded, the riders individually leg yield to the smaller arena and canter onto 10-metre circles at the A and C ends.

They decrease this 10-metre circle and ride forward to walk. From walk, leg yield out to increase the circle and canter a 10-metre circle.

The riders go large onto the small arena and when there is a space, leg yield back to the large arena track and ride forward to trot upon reaching it.

Riders may watch for a space and then leg yield into the small arena to start the exercise again.

NOTES:

Mark the smaller arena and the 10-metre circles with cones.

Notes

Changing Rein Double Arena

gait	**Trot**
difficulty	**ʊʊ**
no. of riders	**6 +**

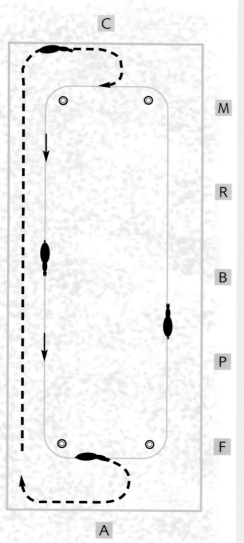

AIMS:

Awareness

Rhythm

To improve changes of flexion and bend

INSTRUCTIONS:

The ride approaches C on the right rein. They individually ride an inwards half 10-metre circle to the small arena.

Upon reaching the small arena the ride tracks left.

Ride either half or full small arena before riding an outwards half circle to the large arena track.

NOTES:

The ride may take sitting trot on the small arena and rising trot on the large arena.

The ride may lengthen the strides between the V–S and the R–P markers.

Riders must prepare to ride from the half circle at C into a corner on the small arena.

Notes

Changing Gaits Double Arena

gait	**Trot, Canter**
difficulty	♘♘
no. of riders	**6 +**

AIMS:

Awareness

Rhythm

Flexion and bend

INSTRUCTIONS:

The ride approaches C on the right rein in canter. They individually ride an inwards half 10-metre circle to the small arena and ride forward to trot.

Upon reaching the small arena the ride tracks left.

Ride either half or full small arena before riding an outwards half circle to the large arena track.

NOTES:

The ride may take sitting trot on the small arena.

Ensure enough space is available before outwards half circling to the large arena.

Riders must be aware of each other before inwards or outwards half circling.

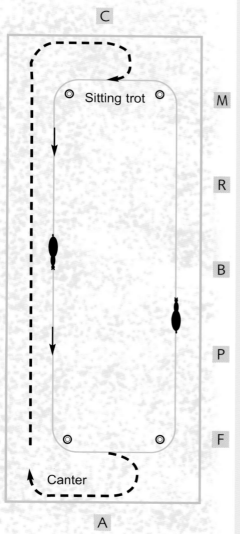

Notes

gait	**Walk, Trot**
difficulty	♘♘
no. of riders	**6 +**

AIMS:

Awareness

Accuracy

Rhythm

INSTRUCTIONS:

At C the ride trots onto a left-rein 10-metre circle.

The ride trots a 30-metre rectangle through X. Add a 10-metre circle at X on the left rein.

Upon reaching B, track right and go large.

Repeat the exercise at the other end of the school.

NOTES:

Riders change rein at B regularly.

If they are too close they can stay on the same rein or ride an extra 10-metre circle.

10-metre circles must be ridden in sitting trot.

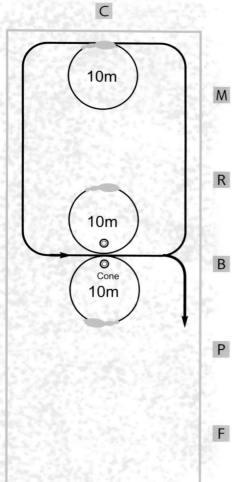

Notes

gait	**Trot, Canter**
difficulty	
no. of riders	**6 +**

AIMS:

Awareness

Transitions

Flexion and bend

INSTRUCTIONS:

At C the ride trots a 10-metre figure of eight.

On completion and in the next corner, canter onto a 30-metre rectangle.

At E trot and turn left straight to B.

At B the ride canters and completes the exercise at the opposite end of the arena.

NOTES:

Advanced riders may ride a simple change at X.

The instructor should check the straightness of the line between E–B.

It may be necessary to mark the figures of eight with cones.

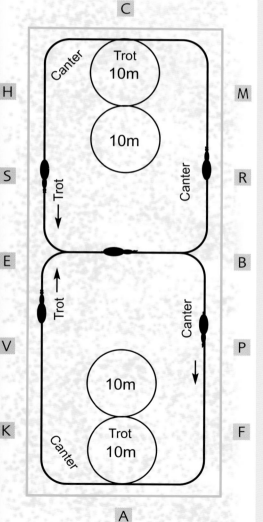

Notes

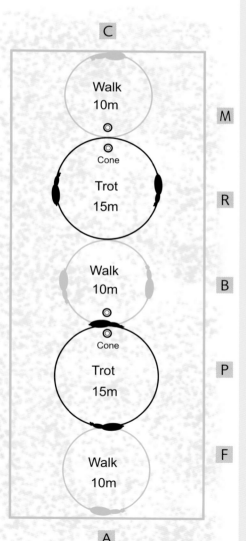

Baby Bubbles

gait	**Walk, Trot**
difficulty	♘
no. of riders	**6 +**

AIM:

Awareness

Flexion and bend

Accuracy

INSTRUCTIONS:

The ride walks a 10-metre circle at C then changes rein and trots a 15-metre circle followed by 10-metre (walk), 15-metre (trot) and finally a 10-metre walk circle.

NOTES:

Place cones to ensure that circles are accurate and properly aligned with the centre line C to A.

Riders must avoid each other when changing circles.

Riders may ride a half circle or 1½ circles depending on the ability of the horse.

Notes

gait	**Walk, Trot**
difficulty	♫
no. of riders	**6 +**

AIM:

Awareness

Improve rising and sitting trot in circles

Flexion

Rhythm

INSTRUCTIONS:

The ride trots onto a 10-metre circle at C in sitting trot and changes rein crossing the centre line to ride a 15-metre circle in rising trot.

The ride continues onto a 10-metre circle sitting trot followed by a 15-metre circle in rising trot until reaching A.

Riders may go large to rest from the circles rejoining this exercise at the other end.

NOTES:

Riders may have to shorten the trot to allow others enough space.

The instructor should place cones to make sure the exercise flows.

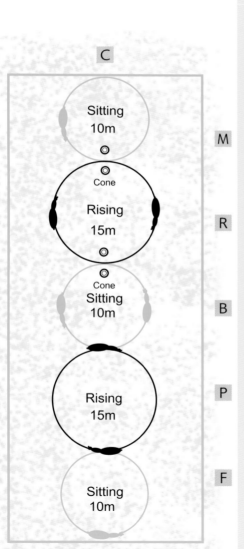

Notes

gait	**Trot**
difficulty	♘♘♘
no. of riders	**6 +**

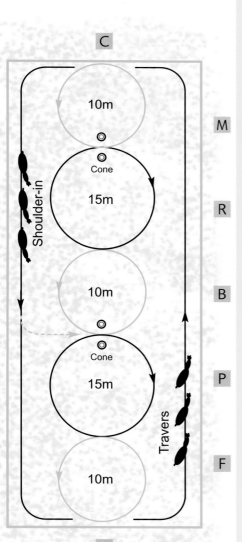

AIM:

Awareness

Flexion and bend

Rhythm

INSTRUCTIONS:

The ride may perform this exercise in sitting trot to work on the changes in flexion and bend without losing rhythm.

The ride may go large down the H–K side and commence shoulder-in.

Or at A ride the ride may ride travers down the F–M side.

NOTES:

Riders in shoulder-in (or travers) may join the middle 10-metre circle if they only wish to ride half the length of the arena.

Notes

for beginner riders

gait	**Trot, Canter**
difficulty	♘
no. of riders	**6 +**

AIM:

Awareness

Flexion and bend

Rhythm

INSTRUCTIONS:

At C the ride canters large along the long side to the first corner.

Upon reaching A the ride trots onto a 10-metre circle, changes rein onto a 15-metre circle and continues on the bubbles until reaching C.

NOTES:

Depending on the level of training, riders may ride either full or half circles before moving to the next one.

C

H

10m
Trot

M

Cone

15m

Trot

S

R

Canter

E

10m
Trot

B

15m

Trot

V

P

K

10m
Trot

F

A

Notes

for novice riders

gait	**Trot, Canter**
difficulty	♘♘
no. of riders	**6 +**

AIM:

Awareness

Flexion and bend

Rhythm

Improve canter and trot transitions

INSTRUCTIONS:

At C the ride canters large to the first corner and trots.

The ride then trots onto a 10-metre circle at A and continues the bubble exercise to the other end of the arena.

NOTES:

Riders may trot the 10-metre circles and canter the 15-metre circles.

The ride must set up the trot transition so it is balanced before the corner and can therefore ride a balanced 10-metre circle.

The riders must prepare for their canter and trot transitions early enough to allow for a smooth, balanced change.

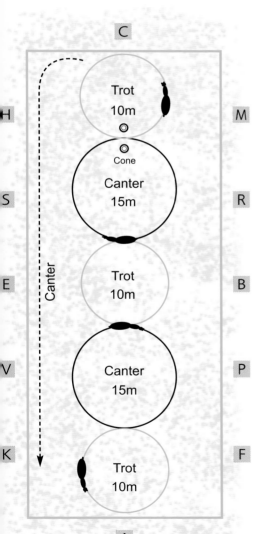

Notes

for advanced riders

gait	**Walk, Trot, Canter**
difficulty	♘♘♘
no. of riders	**6 +**

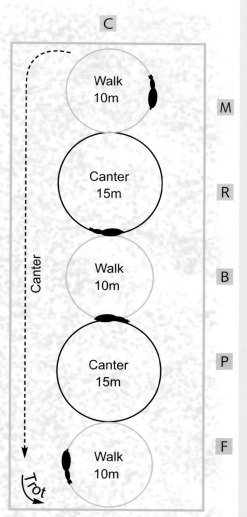

AIM:

Awareness

Transitions

INSTRUCTIONS:

The ride walks 10-metre circles and canters the 15-metre circles.

After completing the bubbles, the ride individually canters down the long sides.

The ride may canter some shoulder-in.

The ride prepares for the transition to the trot before the corner and then walks into the 10-metre circles at A or C.

NOTES:

In the circles, if the canter-walk transitions are not quite balanced, the riders may (remaining safe), decrease the 15-metre circle diameter until the horse is balanced… and give the aid for walk.

Then leg yield out in trot and change rein to walk the next 10-metre circle.

Notes

gait	**Trot, Canter**
difficulty	♘
no. of riders	**6 +**

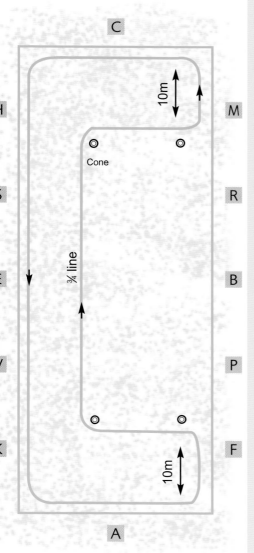

AIM:

Awareness

Flexion and bend

Rhythm

INSTRUCTIONS:

The ride trots around the line of a bubble letter 'C'.

Riders may ride sitting trot on the inside of the 'C' and rising trot on the outside.

When ready the ride may canter large along the outside track near M and return to the trot when reaching F.

NOTES:

Make sure the ride prepares for a balanced transition.

Lengthen or lateral work may be performed down the long side, e.g. shoulder-in.

Notes

Bubble Letters – 'E'

gait	Trot, Canter
difficulty	♘♘
no. of riders	6 +

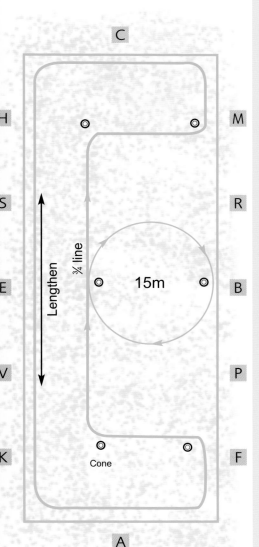

AIM:

Awareness

Balance

Rhythm

INSTRUCTIONS:

First, the ride trots around the line of a bubble letter 'C' (see page 167).

To form the letter 'E', the ride trots a 15-metre circle in the same direction of travel from the E–B line so that it touches the inside of the 'C' and the large arena track at B.

The ride takes rising trot (or canter) on the outside of the letter 'E'.

NOTES:

Place cones so that riders will be precise with the turns and the circle.

Riders may lengthen the stride between S and V.

Notes

gait	**Trot, Canter**
difficulty	♘♘
no. of riders	**6 +**

AIM:

Flexion and bend

Rhythm

Awareness

INSTRUCTIONS:

The ride trots the three-quarter line veering out towards M, looping at C (for two metres) and veering back to the other three-quarter line to form the 'Y'.

NOTES:

The ride may sit trot at the C end of the arena and rise trot for the remainder of the 'Y'.

The ride may lengthen along the diagonal lines of the letter and ride working trot along the straight lines.

The instructor should set up cones as shown.

The ride may also add leg yielding from the three-quarter line to the outside track and then re-join the exercise.

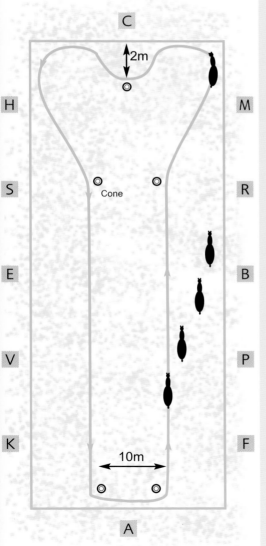

C

↕2m

H

M

S

Cone

R

E

B

V

P

K

F

10m

A

Notes

gait	**Trot, Canter**
difficulty	♘♘
no. of riders	**6 +**

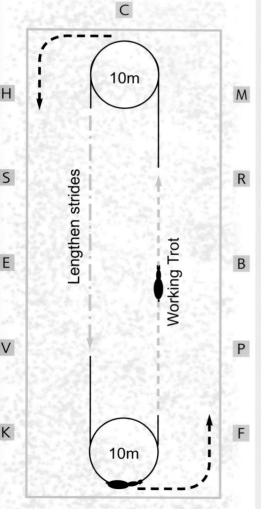

AIM:

Awareness

Training to shorten and lengthen stride within the same rhythm

INSTRUCTIONS:

The ride trot a 10-metre circle at A then rides working trot down the three-quarter line to C followed by a 10-metre circle at C.

Next, they trot down the three-quarter line lengthening the strides to V. This is followed by another 10-metre circle at A.

The ride may go large and rejoin the safety pin at the other end.

NOTES:

The 10-metre circles should be ridden in sitting trot.

The ride may lengthen the trot rising or sitting depending on the level of training.

Use cones to mark the three-quarter lines and 10-metre circles.

Notes

Leg Yield Safety Pin

gait	**Trot**
difficulty	ՍՍ
no. of riders	**6 +**

AIM:

Awareness

Rhythm

INSTRUCTIONS:

The ride trots around the 'Safety Pin' and, when safe, leg yields out to the large arena track rejoining at the other end of the safety pin.

NOTES:

Each rider decides whether to leg yield and must check spacing before moving.

The 10-metre circles must be ridden in sitting trot.

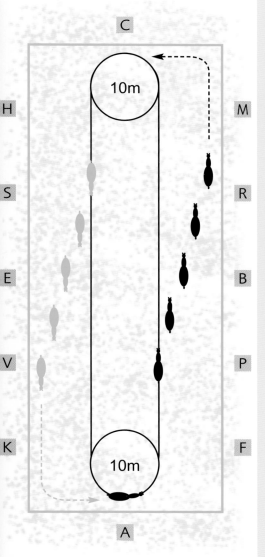

Notes

gait	**Trot, Canter**
difficulty	∪∪
no. of riders	**6 +**

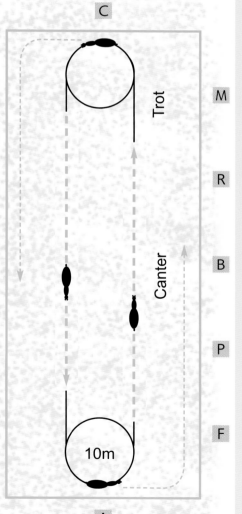

AIM:

Awareness

Transitions

Rhythm

INSTRUCTIONS:

The ride trots into the 'Safety Pin' exercise (see page 173).

The riders individually canter out of the 10-metre circle, along the three-quarter line to the opposite 10-metre circle returning to the trot before entering it.

Riders may also canter the large arena track.

NOTES:

The use of cones will help keep the safety pin straight.

The ride must be prepared for a balanced trot transition before the 10-metre circle.

Notes

gait	**Trot**
difficulty	♘♘
no. of riders	**2–6**

AIM:

Awareness

Flexion and bend

Rhythm

INSTRUCTIONS:

From the right rein at A the ride trots onto the 'bowtie'.

The ride changes rein across the corner line at A and rides into a left 10-metre circle before B.

The ride then trots large on the left rein from B towards C and repeats the exercise in reverse.

NOTES:

Work on maintaining rhythm through the change.

Riders need to watch for each other during the change at B and may have to ride two circles to allow other riders through first.

If the group is larger than six, a second bowtie may be ridden on the other side decreasing the circles to 8 metres.

Use cones to mark the centre line A–C.

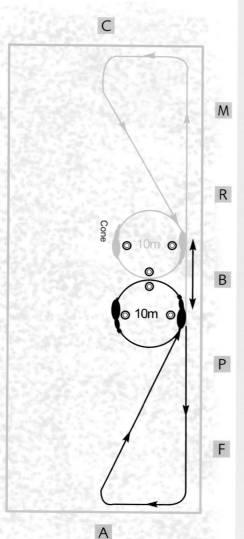

Notes

Lateral Bowtie

gait	**Trot**
difficulty	**ÜÜÜ**
no. of riders	**2–6**

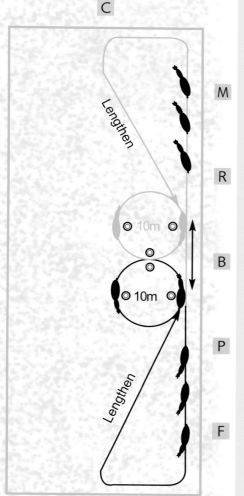

AIM:

Awareness

Flexion and bend

Transitions

INSTRUCTIONS:

At A the ride trots onto the 'bowtie' (see page 179) but with shoulder-in down the long sides and lengthened strides on the diagonal lines with a 10-metre circle before B.

NOTES:

Work on maintaining rhythm through the change.

Riders need to watch for each other during the change at B and may have to ride two circles to allow other riders through first.

If the group is larger than six, a second bowtie may be ridden on the other side of the arena decreasing the circles to 8 metres.

Riders stay on their side of the arena.

The 8-metre circles must be ridden in sitting trot.

Notes

gait	**Walk, Trot**
difficulty	UU
no. of riders	**6 +**

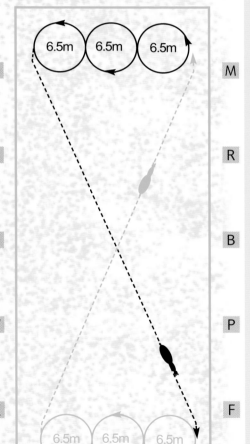

AIM:

Awareness

Changing flexion and bend

Rhythm

INSTRUCTIONS:

At the corner before C ride three 6.5-metre circles completing each circle 1¹/₂ times (OR ride three small serpentine loops).

The ride the diagonal (changing the rein) to repeat the exercise at the other end.

NOTES:

Young riders or horses may ride the circles/serpentines in walk.

Riders must be aware of each other and if collisions become likely at X, ride a few strides along the long side before entering a shortened diagonal.

Notes

Butterfly with Lengthening

gait	**Trot**
difficulty	♘♘
no. of riders	**6 +**

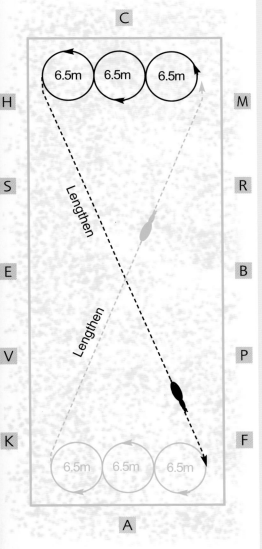

AIM:

Awareness

Flexion and bend

Transitions

INSTRUCTIONS:

Ride onto the butterfly as described on page 183 then lengthen the strides across the diagonal.

Continue the same exercise on the opposite rein.

Work to improve transitions into and out of lengthened trot.

NOTES:

Young riders or horses may ride the circles/serpentines in walk.

Riders must be aware of each other and if collisions become likely at X, ride a few strides along the long side before entering a shortened diagonal.

Notes

gait	**Trot, Canter**
difficulty	♘♘
no. of riders	**2–6**

AIMS:

Awareness

Flexion and bend

Rhythm

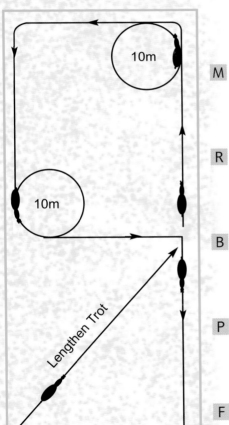

INSTRUCTIONS:

On the left rein after passing B, ride two 10- or 15-metre circles at M and E.

At E cross the centre line to B and track right.

Go large.

At K change rein across the short diagonal lengthening the trot to B.

Upon reaching B continue the exercise.

NOTES:

Any circle may be repeated to allow smooth flow and to avoid collisions.

Give way to lengthening riders.

The circles must be ridden in sitting trot.

This exercise may be ridden at canter with trot across the centre line (E–B).

Notes

gait	**Walk, Trot, Canter**
difficulty	ಅಅಅ
no. of riders	**2–6**

AIMS:

Awareness

Flexion and bend

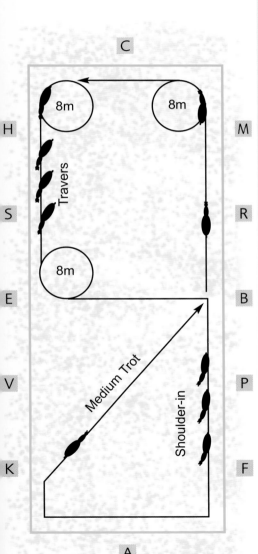

INSTRUCTIONS:

On the left rein after passing B, ride 8-metre circles in the next two corners.

Ride another 8-metre circle at E then cross the centre line to B and track right.

Go large.

At K change rein across the short diagonal in medium trot to B.

Upon reaching B continue the exercise.

Additionally ride left travers from H to E and ride right shoulder-in from B to F.

NOTES:

Riders must ride a straight line from E to B.

The 8-metre circles must be ridden in sitting trot.

The lateral work may all be ridden in shoulder-in if the riders are not ready for travers.

Notes

Index

EXERCISES TO IMPROVE...

Accuracy: 23, 39, 41, 43, 45, 69, 71, 85, 97, 113, 129, 131, 133, 151, 155
Awareness: 23, 25, 31, 39, 41, 43, 45, 47, 49, 51, 53, 55, 57, 59, 61, 63, 65, 67, 71, 73, 81, 85, 87, 91, 93, 95, 97, 99, 107, 111, 113, 121, 123, 125, 127, 131, 135, 137, 139, 141, 143, 145, 147, 149, 151, 153, 155, 157, 159, 161, 163, 165, 167, 169, 171, 173, 175, 177, 179, 181, 183, 185, 187, 189
Balance: 57, 59, 63, 73, 79, 81, 95, 97, 103, 125, 141, 169
Canter work: 55, 57, 61, 65, 69, 71, 73, 77, 79, 83, 89, 97, 113, 115, 117, 119, 123, 131, 143, 149, 161, 165, 169, 171, 173, 177
Corners: 49, 97, 99, 141
Flexion and bend: 39, 41, 43, 45, 47, 49, 51, 53, 55, 57, 59, 61, 87, 89, 91, 93, 95, 101, 135, 137, 147, 149, 153, 155, 157, 159, 161, 163, 167, 171, 179, 181, 183, 185, 187, 189
    changes of bend: 51, 53, 55, 59, 61, 91, 93, 95, 137, 147, 183
Half circles: 29, 31
Half halt: 33
Halts: 25, 27, 29, 121, 123, 125, 135
Hands: 77
Lateral work: 63, 79, 81, 99, 105, 107, 109, 111
    leg yield: 79, 81, 109, 111, 127, 133, 137, 141, 143, 145, 171, 175
    shoulder-in: 99, 125, 189
    travers: 125, 189
    turn on the forehand: 105, 107
Lengthened trot: 67, 123, 125, 139, 169, 171, 173, 181, 185, 187
Preparation: 37, 65, 107, 125, 137
Rein-back: 25
Rhythm: 35, 47, 49, 51, 53, 55, 57, 67, 69, 87, 89, 91, 101, 103, 109, 111, 115, 117, 129, 131, 133, 143, 145, 147, 149, 151, 157, 159, 161, 163, 167, 169, 171, 175, 177, 179, 183, 187
Safety: 23, 59, 61, 63
Sitting trot: 93, 137, 149, 157
Straightness: 23, 27, 119, 123, 129, 133, 143
Transitions: 21, 31, 35, 39, 41, 43, 53, 55, 65, 67, 71, 73, 75, 81, 83, 89, 99, 113, 115, 117, 121, 123, 125, 127, 135, 139, 143, 145, 153, 163, 165, 177, 181, 185;
    walk/trot: 31, 35, 75, 127
    halt/trot: 121, 123, 125, 135
    trot/canter: 43, 65, 67, 71, 73, 75, 89, 115, 143, 153, 163, 177
    walk/canter: 83, 123, 145, 165

Notes